TIME-BLOCKING

Your Method to Supercharge Productivity
& Reach Your Goals

LUKE SEAVERS

One Nine Pro Publishing

CHARLESTON, SC

Copyright © 2020 by **Luke Seavers**

All rights reserved. No part of this publication may be reproduced, distributed or transmitted in any form or by any means, without prior written permission.

One Nine Pro Publishing
www.oneninepro.com

Book Design by Luke Seavers
Edited by Cortney Donelson
Author Headshot by Sarah Elaine Photography

Time-Blocking: Your Method to Supercharge Productivity & Reach Your Goals / **Luke Seavers**. -- 1st ed.

ISBN: 9798588777780

Scripture taken from the Holy Bible, New International Version®, NIV®.
Copyright © 1973, 1978, 1984, 2011 by Biblica, Inc.™
Used by permission of Zondervan. All rights reserved worldwide.
www.zondervan.com
The "NIV" and "New International Version" are trademarks registered in the United States Patent and Trademark Office by Biblica, Inc.™

To my Mastermind Group
THOMAS HEATH, JON STROUD, & LISA BURBAGE
for keeping me accountable to get this book done.

&

To my wife
SEMONE
for always supporting me and encouraging me
in everything I do.

CONTENTS

Introduction 1

The Time-Blocking Mindset 7

Chapter 1: Maintain Single-Focus 9
Chapter 2: Determine Your Essentials 17
Chapter 3: Achieve More by Doing Less 29
Chapter 4: Plan to Recharge 39
Chapter 5: Take Back Control of Your Time 47

The Time-Blocking Method 61

Chapter 6: Macro-Blocking 63
Chapter 7: Micro-Blocking 77
Chapter 8: Day-Blocking (Part I) 87
Chapter 9: Day-Blocking (Part II) 115

Final Thoughts 133

INTRODUCTION

There's just not enough time in the day...

I would consider myself to be a driven person. I'm an entrepreneur with many dreams and goals that I long to see accomplished in my life, even in this year alone. But with this, has often come the familiar frustration: *there's just not enough time in the day.*

It felt as if I had uttered this lament on more occasions than I could count. This time, I was in the kitchen venting to my wife after a long day. Sure, I had gotten several things checked off my To-Do list that day, but I just wasn't able to get to all the things I had planned to do.

But my wife, of course, met me with a familiar reply: "Well, you know, everyone is given the exact same twenty-four hours each day."

This had never seemed that helpful–it certainly wasn't at this moment. In fact, it only served to fuel my frustration.

Why couldn't I get everything done that I wanted to get done? Was I doing something wrong?

Was I not working hard *enough?* It sure felt like I couldn't work much harder than I already was.

Was I not working long *enough?* I was already burning the candle at both ends, plus working many weekends.

What was I missing?

As much as it pained me to say, when it came down to it, I had to admit that my wife was right. Every one of the all-time "greats"—individuals such as Thomas Edison, Oprah Winfrey, Steve Jobs, J.K. Rowling, and Michael Jordan—were all given the same amount of time each day to accomplish incredible things. Each of these men and women, on top of all the others you could name, had just twenty-four hours.

One thing was for sure: whether winning an NBA championship or building a multi-billion-dollar business, they did something right. They took the twenty-four hours they were given and maximized it to their greatest ends. I would venture to guess they managed their time well.

When we talk about productivity, the conversation often goes to time management. How can we manage our time better? But what if I told you that the secret to productivity was actually not managing your time.

Time is a limited resource. It's constantly slipping by, with no way to retrieve it. And though we can learn to manage the little time that we have, we will still never be able to get more of it. The expression we use to "make more time for __" is ultimately a lie.

So, you see, the secret to productivity is not managing your time but managing your *focus*.

What we can do is find ways to increase our capacity to focus, and use *this* to maximize the time we are given.

Of course, to say that the answer to all of your productivity woes is "focus management" is like saying the secret to winning the Super Bowl is by playing football well. What you need is a game plan.

Time-Blocking *is* your game plan for effectively managing not just your time, but, more importantly, your focus. It will allow you to achieve new levels of productivity and reach your highest goals.

When I first discovered this productivity superweapon, I was skeptical of it. The idea of planning out my entire day hour-by-hour initially seemed too constraining. I was also concerned that spending the extra time to "Time-Block" my day would end up taking valuable time away from me. But what I have found is that it has provided me more freedom, not less. I eventually learned how to do it in less than a minute on any given day.

I see now why this tool has been utilized in some form by accomplished individuals, including Elon Musk and Bill Gates.[i]

During my first year using this method, I managed to reach ninety percent of the goals I had set for that year. Yes, ninety percent! (The missed ten percent was due, in part, to circumstances beyond my control and, in part, to setting one very unrealistic goal). Among these goals were finalizing my daughter's adoption, joining a growing tech startup putting in over 200 hours of sweat equity, raising $12,000 dollars for a project to bring water to remote villages in Haiti, and taking three vacations—all while continuing to run my branding and marketing agency and remaining present as a husband and a father.

The Time-Blocking Method can be used to win your day, giving you the focus you need to manage large tasks, reduce daily distractions, and complete your To-Do list in less time.

It will allow you to accomplish long-term professional goals, such as launching a product, meeting monthly sales quotas, or writing a book. (This book was written using the Time-Blocking Method.) You can use it to learn a foreign language, schedule daily prayer and meditation, train for a marathon, or master a musical instrument.

It can even help you improve your relationships, giving you *more* time and *better quality* time with your children, spouse, or close friends. It is for business owners, employees, CEOs, managers, athletes, artists, stay-at-home-moms, and more.

Time-Blocking is not a magic formula. In fact, it's actually a simple concept.

If I shared just the bare bones method with you, I could probably explain it in just a page or two. But I feel that I would be doing you a massive disservice.

You see, you could go and start Time-Blocking today and begin filling up your schedule with loads of tasks. You may even see that you are getting a lot of *things* done. But let's make an important distinction here. Getting a lot of things done does not necessarily mean you are achieving productivity. It probably means you're achieving busyness.

Chances are, you are already busy. You are too busy right now to accomplish all of the things you want to accomplish. Busyness has gotten you nowhere up until this point, and it should not be the end goal. What I am about to teach you in this book is how to be truly productive, not busy.

And for this reason, I am not only going to teach you the Time-Blocking Method, but also explain the *mindset* behind it. In Section 1, we will dig deep into the "Time-Blocking Mindset." This is the philosophy behind why it works, as well as the approach you need to take in order to be successful with it.

Throughout these first few chapters, we will discuss the Five Rules of Time-Blocking, which are:

1. Maintain Single-Focus
2. Determine Your Essentials
3. Achieve More by Doing Less
4. Plan to Recharge
5. Take Back Control of Your Time

After this, we will do a deep dive into the actual Time-Blocking Method, discussing the three different ways to Time-Block: (1) Macro-Blocking, (2) Micro-Blocking, and (3) Day-Blocking.

I will teach you how to implement these methods, looking at specific examples, and follow an effective process for planning your day, your week, and your year. We recommend picking up a copy of *The Time-Blocking Day Planner*, available at timeblockingbook.com, which accompanies these steps.

Are you ready to supercharge productivity, and reach your goals? Then, let's jump in!

SECTION I

the TIME-BLOCKING MINDSET

CHAPTER ONE

MAINTAIN SINGLE-FOCUS

If I had to use one word to describe our "first-world" culture, it would be busy.

Busyness is so ingrained in our way of life that we wear it as a badge of honor. Think about it: you run into a friend or colleague, who asks you, "How are things? . . . How's work . . . How's business?"

And our response? "Busy."

Now, partially, our answer is our subtle admission of the stressful life that we live. But the other half of us feels a small sense of pride when we say this. Though we loathe our stress, we're also addicted to it.

And it's clear that others around us see it the same way. Without fail, anytime I've given this reply, the person who initially asked responds with something like, "Well that's a good thing, right? Better than not being busy."

But is this true? Is busyness a good thing?

Having spent time living abroad in a developing country, I perhaps have established a bit of a different perspective on this.

In other parts of the world, for example, Latin America, Africa, and Haiti (where I lived), life can be hard, but I would never describe it as busy.

The pace of life in these places is slower, the concept of being "on-time" is a bit subjective, and the people tend to value time spent on relationships more than on tasks. There is actually something very refreshing about this. If anything, it's shown me there is a different way of thinking beyond what we experience in our culture. It has shown me that busyness is not necessarily a virtue.

Even if you already agree with me, chances are you've come to accept busyness as a necessary evil. To reach your goals, there's no other way. You have to hustle and grind if you are ever going to accomplish them. Trust me, I fully support the "hustle" and I know the value of putting in the hard work; but might I suggest to you that working harder (and the busyness that comes with it) should not be the goal?

If we're not careful, we can get used to our busyness and feel a sense of accomplishment in it, without actually getting anything of value done.

If you're reading this book, there is a good chance that your hard work has only taken you so far. There is another way! To achieve the outcomes that really matter to you, you need to begin to think differently. Stop seeing hard work as an end in itself. Stop being content with a busy life, and aim for a meaningful life, using productivity as your vehicle.

The Time-Blocking Mindset is one that aims for true productivity. Productivity is about working smart. If you want, you can use Time-Blocking to "work smarter, not harder." However, I'm a big proponent of working smarter and harder. It's totally up to you how you choose to apply it.

THE SECRET TO PRODUCTIVITY

The secret sauce behind true productivity—and what makes Time-Blocking so effective—is *focus*.

Focus is something of a commodity in our day and age. You have to admit that we live in a revolutionary time in history. With smartphones, online video, e-learning, social media, etc., we've never had so many resources at our disposal, and we've never been so connected to our fellow human beings. It really is an amazing time to live in.

But amidst all of these advancements, I'm afraid one of the major things that has suffered in our society is our focus. To say that we are simply distracted would be oversimplifying the issue. What is really happening is that our focus is divided in a million directions, and we have adapted in such a way that this is the new norm.

When I say that focus is a commodity, what I mean is that it is an actual currency that we are spending way too frivolously. Just like money, it is something we need to learn to manage.

When we feel we are being unproductive, conventional wisdom instructs us to figure out how we can manage our time better. But in reality, what is more beneficial is learning to manage our focus, and the rest will follow.

MULTI-TASKING VS. SINGLE-FOCUS

In order to make the Time-Blocking Method work, you need to come to grips with the truth that *multitasking doesn't work*.

On the surface, multitasking may seem like such an obvious productivity hack. It's the idea that the more you can juggle at once, the more you get done. We have ascribed to this belief so much that companies will even hire so-called "multitaskers" over individuals who admit to having a harder time at it.

The problem is that it's a lie that multitasking is a useful skill. In fact, the supposed ability to multitask is not what its name suggests. Research[ii] tells us that what is actually occurring is our brain is switching rapidly between these multiple tasks, to the point where it appears simultaneous, but in reality, our brain is only able to handle one task at a time.

This was illustrated in a study[iii] conducted on the Western Washington University campus, where students and pedestrians were observed walking through the campus square. Dr. Ira Hyman and his psychology students inserted a unicycling clown into the middle of the square, a particularly unusual spectacle to see on a college campus. Passerbyers were asked if they had noticed anything out-of-the-ordinary after walking through the square, and most notably, of those who had been walking and talking on their cell phone, only eight percent could recall anything unusual. When asked directly if they had seen the unicycling clown, still only twenty-five percent said they saw the clown.

Dr. Hyman notes that though these students likely put their eyes on the clown, they didn't actually "see" it. At that moment, their brain was fixated on their phone conversations, not on their surroundings.

Texting and driving provides us with a similar example. Many people recognize this to be generally a bad idea, and most U.S. states have prohibited it entirely. Though we know that it is physically possible to text and drive a car at the same time, it is impossible to focus fully on both tasks. During those few moments composing a quick reply while cruising down the interstate, you are no longer focused on the road. The only reason you can physically accomplish the driving portion is because of the muscle memory you've developed from years of driving. That does not mean your brain is actually cognizant of everything happening on the road. We all know that it only takes one sudden stop from the car in front of us for none of this to matter. Your muscle memory can only get you so far. Only a focused driver can avoid getting into a wreck.

Not only is multitasking virtually a myth, attempting it is extremely harmful to your productivity. That's because it works against our goal of *focus*.

Lack of focus can be costly. In situations like the example above, it can endanger your life and the lives of others. But when it comes to daily tasks and activities, it can cost you both your time and energy. And in doing so it may eventually cost you your dreams and ambitions.

In college, I used to volunteer at a local nursing home, spending time with the residents, listening to their stories. If you want some perspective on your life, you may also want to pay these folks a visit. There, you will meet many pleasant people, but you will also encounter many regret-ridden individuals—those nearing the ends of their lives, wishing they had more time to do what they had dreamed to do. Others, wishing they had more *time* to spend with the people they care about. But I would wager time was never the real issue, but rather, a lack of focus in their lives.

Focus is a precious resource. And one of the biggest ways you can start managing your focus is to stop multitasking immediately.

You cannot give 100 percent to even two activities at once. The math just doesn't add up. One of those things is going to suffer, and in most cases, both will.

Now, you may be thinking, "OK, I understand that you can't give 100 percent to two tasks at once, but I'm still giving fifty percent to two tasks in twice the amount of time, so it all pans out."

But this is not the case. What you're not taking into account is the toll of task-switching. We will be discussing this more in a future chapter, but switching from one unrelated task to another takes more of a mental strain on us than we realize. Due to the mental energy exerted from shifting our focus, we are actually spending extra time we don't need to be spending.

Not only is it impossible to give 100 percent to two things at once, it's also true that you can't give your all to one single task when there are other things fighting for your attention.

Let's say your current objective for the hour is to send a proposal off to a client, but while you're working on that, you're also listening to your favorite band on shuffle and periodically replying to your coworkers on Slack. With these three different things pulling your attention back and forth, you cannot expect to get that proposal done quickly.

At any given time, your focus is only going to be on one of those things. You may be *hearing* the music, but you are not actively listening to it (i.e. giving it your focus) while you are concentrated on your proposal. But at any point, your favorite song might come on, and all of a sudden, you are jamming out, contemplating the meaning of the lyrics, or reliving the nostalgia of the first time you heard the song. Your focus has shifted away from your main task.

Or your co-worker pings you to ask about some project, one unrelated to the proposal you're trying to complete. Again, you are forced to shift your focus to address their issue. Then, yet again, you must shift your focus back to what you were doing.

The beauty of Time-Blocking is that it is a tool to help prevent this and manage your focus well. But first, you must commit to stop multitasking. More importantly, you need to replace this bad habit with the right habit:

Rule #1 of Time-Blocking is to *maintain single-focus.*

The opposite of multi-tasking is *single-focus*ing. Notice, I did not use the term "single-tasking" as the antagonist to multitasking. That's because I don't believe it is enough to think of this only in terms of work-related tasks. The issue of focusing on more than one thing at a time does not only plague our work but all areas of our lives.

Maintaining single-focus will be a fundamental mind shift from the way you currently view the world. I believe to fully apply this to your daily tasks, you deserve to make a change in every facet of your life.

For many of you who consider yourself to be good multitaskers, this may be a harder shift for you to make. But what you need to realize is you're actually sabotaging yourself and hurting your productivity.

If you are like me and you didn't consider yourself to be a good multitasker to begin with, it will still be a challenge. It has been a difficult habit for me to kick (and I am still not perfect at it). Because multitasking has become such a coveted ability in our culture, I never realized how often I tried to multitask in different areas of my life.

It has taken a lot of unlearning. So, I decided that, in order to stop multitasking at work, I needed to quit doing it in all areas of my life. I needed to put down the phone and stop browsing social media while at the dinner table with my family. I needed to stop doing work during time that was meant for play. I began making it my goal to be more present and not dwell on issues that had nothing to do with the present moment. This is what I continue to strive for, anyway.

I would encourage you to consider taking similar steps and apply this Time-Blocking Mindset to every area of your life. This will help you to start to unlearn your multitasking habit, and you may be amazed by how this simple act of maintaining single-focus transforms your life.

THE CURE FOR BUSYNESS

We started off this chapter talking about our addiction to being busy. Without realizing it, we have fooled ourselves into thinking we're productive, when in reality, we're just busy.

Busyness is directly correlated to our lack of focus. The busy, unproductive person is the multitasker who has his focus divided in several directions at once. The productive person is the one who has a single focus at any given moment. But it is not enough to focus on just anything.

In the next chapter, we will discuss the specifics of what you should be focusing on when Time-Blocking.

CHAPTER TWO

DETERMINE YOUR ESSENTIALS

When I was in school, I remember some of the ridiculous homework my teachers assigned us. There was one year in elementary school when we were assigned a "Tree Report." Now, I went to a small private school, so I really have no idea if this is a typical school project or not; but as I recall, we were supposed to choose a tree in our backyard and document it for the entire school year. Talk about *watching grass grow*! Month after month, I struggled to fudge a new two-page report on the exciting "changes" that occurred in this fully-grown tree. I think I had to draw a new picture of it each month, and staple leaves on a page in a three-ringed binder.

I thought, "This is just busywork." Even as a kid, I was frustrated with the fact my time was being wasted, and I didn't think I was learning anything new in the process.

So then, why, as adults, do we inflict the same torture on ourselves? Why are we constantly assigning ourselves busywork?

BURN YOUR TO-DO LIST

Not all tasks are created equal. Deep down we know this, but our actions say otherwise.

Since starting my business, I have become a list maker. Adding tasks to a To-Do list has been a way to cope with the endless responsibilities that come with running a business.

To-Do lists have their place. They can help us stay on top of daily tasks and remember important tasks for later. For many of us productivity nerds, it can be exhilarating when that moment comes when we draw a big check mark next to that item or cross it off our list. That sense of accomplishment we feel can often lead us to believe we are being super productive. But should it?

If you are like I was, and you keep checking things off your To-Do list (whether it be a mental list or an actual, physical one), yet still feel as if there is not enough time in the day to do what you set out to do, then I can guarantee you that you're not being as productive as you think.

The truth is most of our days are filled with busywork. And it shouldn't come as a surprise that when we focus on the busywork, we find ourselves constantly busy.

The problem is we don't know how to distinguish the important tasks from the unimportant ones when they're all mixed together in the same list. And when we view everything as important then *nothing* is.

This is why our traditional To-Do lists aren't going to cut it if we are going to supercharge productivity and reach our goals. The Time-Blocking Method is a replacement for your To-Do list of busywork. Yes, it is a To-Do list of sorts, but it's a more intentional one, focused on the essential tasks. That's why:

Rule #2 of Time-Blocking is to *determine your essentials*.

WHAT DO YOU VALUE?

Greg McKeown coined the term "Essentialism," and in his book of the same name, he states,

> *The way of the Essentialist means living by design, not by default. Instead of making choices reactively, the Essentialist deliberately distinguishes the vital few from the trivial many, eliminates the nonessentials, and then removes obstacles so the essential things have clear, smooth passage.*[iv]

But many of us have not taken the time to truly articulate what is most essential in our lives.

For starters, what is your *calling*? What is your *life's purpose*? Author and TED speaker, Simon Sinek, calls this your "Why." He says that while everyone knows *what* they do, and many can also define *how* they do it, very few can answer the question of *why* they do what they do. To echo the words of Mark Twain, "The two most important days in your life are the day you are born and the day you find out why."

To determine our essentials, we need to start with this foundational question because, without it, we will continue living our lives by default. We can implement the Time-Blocking Method all we want, but without a sense of purpose and intentionality, we will only be achieving productivity for productivity's sake.

Not only that, but the sheer ability to *get a lot of stuff done* is not ultimately going to provide you with the motivation you need to keep moving forward. You need to answer the question for yourself, "Why am I even doing any of this?" so that at the end of your productivity journey, you can look back and see that it was all for something bigger than yourself.

I recognize this is no small question, and for those who have never pondered it before, I wouldn't expect you to have an answer now; but I hope you will start on a journey to learn your purpose.

Often connected with this larger question, is the question of, *What are the things that you value most?* Right now, most of us could easily articulate that we value things like family, relationships, creativity, hard work, making money, self-care, God, religion, giving back, or enjoying life. But these concepts, unfortunately, are way too vague, and ultimately, unhelpful to provide any real direction in your life.

These so-called "values" could be applied to anyone and everyone. They are not specific enough to you. For instance, if you say you value relationships, what do you mean? Relationships with whom? Everyone you meet on the street? Your coworkers? Your spouse? All of your Facebook friends? Your best friend?

The truth is you don't actually value *all* relationships. My guess is, when you say you value relationships, you have a select few people in mind. You know that trying to build a friendship with everyone you meet would be unrealistic. For the most outgoing person, it would be impossible, even if you tried. That's because if you invested an equal amount of energy into every person you know, then all of your relationships—especially your closest ones—would suffer. By making every relationship in your life important, you make *none* of them important.

So, you have to get specific about the *thing* in which you value. Again, you most likely already know, but I would encourage you take a moment to articulate those specifics and write them down.

But let's take it a step deeper. You may say that you value your relationship with your spouse or significant other. That's great! But if you never go on dates with them, buy them gifts, or say nice things to them, one might question how much you really value that relationship.

Values aren't just ethereal concepts. They are backed up by actions.

It is often the execution of said action that can be challenging. I love my wife, and I know that she especially needs to hear words of affirmation in order to feel loved by me. But if I'm honest, showing love in this way can be tough for me, and I don't always execute it very well. For this reason, I want you to not only define the specific *thing* you value but also a specific action or goal that goes with it. Using the example of my relationship with my wife: If I am going to show love to my wife, my goal needs to be to speak encouraging words to her every day.

Or let's say that one of the values you've articulated is that you want to make more money while working less hours so you can spend more time with your family. How can you convert this value into a goal? Perhaps it means you need to create some sort of passive stream of income, or it may mean you need to ask your boss for a raise and the opportunity to work from home. These are just examples of potential goals that line up with your values, and they will be different from person to person.

When it comes to goal-setting, we would do well to use a slightly modified version of Peter Drucker's "SMART Goals" as a guide. Any goal we set should be:

1. Specific
2. Measurable
3. Actionable
4. Realistic
5. Time-Bound

(As my colleague Thomas Heath has pointed out to me, the original SMART Goals used the word "Attainable" as letter **A**; however, this should already be a given. He prefers using "Actionable" here, as this is serves as a better guide for setting goals we can easily convert to actionable steps, and I completely agree.)

REVERSE ENGINEERING

In 1982, IBM dominated the personal computer landscape with their IBM-PC being the best-selling in the world at the time. While there were many IBM-PC copycats at the time, none of them lived up to the success of their predecessor because most of the software being developed at the time was only compatible with IBM's machine.

However, it was also at that time that Rod Canion and two other mid-level managers at Texas Instruments saw the opportunity to set out on their own to compete with the tech giant. Canion and his associates sought to create a portable computer you could travel with, but they knew, in order for them to be successful, their machine would need to be 100 percent IBM-PC compatible, making it more accessible to the general public. To do this was no easy task because they could not simply use IBM's copyrighted code. In fact, if any of their developers even looked at the original code, it could put them at risk for a lawsuit.

What they did to get around this was sheer genius. They underwent a process to "reverse engineer" IBM's software. This process involved looking at the high-level view of what the original software did, break that down into smaller processes, repeat again and again, and then, starting from scratch, write code that would be able to accomplish the same functions. The process was long and tedious, but later that year, the team launched its flagship product, the Compaq Portable. It was the first 100 percent PC-compatible computer in the world and a huge success.[v]

To determine your essentials, you need to follow a similar process with your life. Take a look at the life you are trying to create for yourself–your life's goals–and reverse engineer the steps to get there. In doing so, the process of reverse engineering your life will allow you to know what tasks you should be Time-Blocking.

You see, simply setting a goal isn't enough. There is a reason we have trouble following through on the things we are most passionate about.

Oftentimes, our goals feel too big, and we don't know where to start. And even when we do figure out where to start and hit the ground running, that initial momentum often only carries us so far. As we begin taking action on our goals, we start to see how much effort is actually involved, and it can overwhelm us. Before learning the philosophy behind Time-Blocking, I can't tell you how many projects I started, getting twenty-five percent, fifty percent, and sometimes even seventy-five percent done, and then eventually losing steam and never completing it.

Reverse engineering your goals is a way to create a roadmap to follow through to the end. It is a simple exercise of breaking your goal into steps. And then taking those steps and breaking them up into smaller steps. Then taking those and breaking them into even smaller steps. And so on.

Now, you may be thinking, "But that is only going to make me more overwhelmed, seeing my goal broken up into a million steps." You're not wrong. And this is where you must determine how important the goal is to you. Is this goal really an essential goal?

It's also possible it's not a goal for *now*. You may see it as an essential goal to reach in the next five years, the next ten, or just sometime in your lifetime; but it's not a goal for *today*.

But don't worry, the primary purpose of reverse engineering your goal is actually not to overwhelm you. With the right goal—one that is essential—you will come away empowered. It will result in a realistic plan you can start taking action on right away.

In Section 2 of this book, I show you how Time-Blocking provides a framework for reverse engineering your goals and "blocking" the tasks associated with them. I will show you how to apply this to both large, long-term goals, as well as small, daily goals.

MAKING THE TRADEOFF

Not all tasks are created equal, and by continuing to view all the tasks on our To-Do list as equal, I fear we are destined for a life of frustration and unfulfilled dreams. We may wake up one day and realize that our life has passed us by, and we wasted it.

Stop allowing the high of "getting stuff done" deceive you into believing you're being productive.

What we must do is determine the essential tasks and give them our focus. It is the only way you will have success with Time-Blocking. If you Time-Block every hour of your day but don't achieve the most important tasks, reach your goals, and achieve your highest purpose, then what good is it?

What you need to understand is that saying "yes" to the essential tasks, requires saying "no" to almost all others. This is the reality of tradeoffs. We often want it both ways, but this is just not possible.

No is not a dirty word. Some reading this will have the most trouble saying "no" to other people (don't worry we'll get to that!). But for others—myself included—the most difficult "no" you'll have to give is to yourself. And while you may believe you can do anything you set your mind to, there is a caveat to this. In reality, you can only do one thing you set your mind to do at any given time. (Remember, multitasking doesn't work). So you must accept that in order to go "all in" with your essentials, you must be willing to make the necessary tradeoffs.

Now you may be thinking, "How can I say 'No' to busywork tasks I'm expected to do?" To answer this, you need to discern whether those tasks are truly essential or not.

If failing to complete a task would result in you losing your job or losing a key client, then I would consider that to be fairly essential (assuming that one of your values is to have a job or maintain a thriving business). But you want to make it a habit of questioning whether each task meets your requirements for an essential task, rather than just blindly tackling your To-Do list. Always ask yourself, "If I put off this task or don't complete it altogether, what would happen?" Sure, there will likely be some repercussions, but how severe would they be? Are they actually life shattering, or will the damage be minimal?

Author Tim Farris, in an article entitled, "The Art of Letting Bad Things Happen," says, "Oftentimes, in order to do the big things, you have to let the small bad things happen."[vi] Farris concurs that attention (i.e. *focus*) should be valued over *time*, and if we are to direct our focus to the most important things in life, we have to let some to-dos fall by the wayside.

If you happened to drive by my house at just the wrong time, you would probably notice a yard in disarray—with weeds springing up all over the place and, occasionally, grass the height of your knees. This is my fault, of course, as it's my responsibility to take care of my property. Though I have to admit that I'm somewhat embarrassed by the fact, mostly I'm *OK* with it.

Having a nice yard, frankly, is just not high enough on my list of values. Sure, I would love to have an immaculately landscaped property all the time. However, when I look at time and energy required to mow and keep it up every single week compared to the opportunity to spend it on more essential tasks, it often leads me to put it off. This is a trade-off I am willing to make as I would much rather direct that time and energy toward things like building my business or playing with my kids. Ultimately, I can accept the repercussions of an ugly yard: the judgment of others, occasional complaints from the neighbors, and *me* having to look at the eye-sore that is my lawn day after day. In the grand scheme of things, it's not the end of the world.

Something else to consider is, just because a task is essential, doesn't mean it's an essential task for *you* to complete. If a task is taking away time—and more importantly, focus—from the essential tasks only *you* can do, find ways to delegate. As often as I can, I'm happy to hire landscapers to take the yardwork off my plate. I'm not someone who believes "a man should mow his own lawn." Nor do I believe that the woman of the house has to clean her own home. For most businesses, continuing to do every nitty gritty task yourself will eventually stifle your growth. If you have the means to do so, outsource and delegate the non-essential tasks so you can focus on the essential ones.

There will always be tradeoffs. To focus on your essentials, you will need to be OK with saying no and possibly neglecting something only mildly important to choose the best "yes."

In the next chapter, we will take this concept a step further to learn how we can achieve *more* by doing *less*.

.

CHAPTER THREE

ACHIEVE MORE BY DOING LESS

So far, we've talked about why you need to maintain single-focus in your work... and in all areas of life, for that matter. To do this, you need to determine your essentials. This starts with articulating your essential values, which you can translate into essential goals, which you can then reverse engineer into your essential tasks.

These essential tasks are what we should be filling our days with. In this chapter, we are going to talk about how you should go about doing this.

"SAID IT" AND FORGET IT

Saying "Yes" to the essential tasks, and "No" to the non-essentials is easier said than done.

Throughout our day, we are constantly thinking up new things we "need" to get done, not to mention the outside requests of the "Honey Do" list or extra assignments from our bosses. As this checklist grows, it gets harder to prioritize our essential tasks when we are bogged down and overwhelmed by everything all at once. And more often than not, we resort to doing the task as soon as we think of it in an effort not to forget about it.

What we need to create is a *Said It and Forget It* List. This is essentially the anti-To-Do List. With this list, we write down any and every task that pops into our heads. Most To-Do lists stop here and become just that: a list of ideas that pop into our heads. But the purpose of this list is not necessarily to get any of these tasks done. The purpose is to take them off our minds.

There is a benefit to writing things down. When you merely keep a mental checklist, your brain is needing to use extra energy (i.e. *focus*) in order to remember and keep track of everything that needs to be done. These mental To-Do lists are even more harmful than our paper To-Do lists. They become a mixture of today's tasks scrambled with the tasks we need to remember for tomorrow or the following week. It is needless, and even harmful to our psyche, to have tomorrow's tasks on our minds today. As Jesus told his followers, "Do not worry about tomorrow . . . each day has enough trouble of its own."[vii]

As soon as you write down a task, your mind is able to relax because it no longer has to do the work of remembering that task. You can take your mind off of it and focus better on the task at hand.

The *Said It and Forget It List* is for this very purpose. Any time we think of a new task, we write it down. Writing tasks down gives us a bird's eye view. We're able to think clearer and more objectively about them, helping us better determine the ones that deserve our focus.

Once we've compiled our list, our next step is probably the most crucial: we need to get rid of our *Said It and Forget It*

List—out of sight, out of mind. To deter us from working on the tasks on this list, we have put it somewhere, away from our view as we go through our day.

If we wanted to, we could completely throw away this list, chuck it in the trash. Think about it; if we have determined our truly essential tasks, do we need to worry about this list anymore? The only reason I don't recommend setting fire to your list (at least, not right away) is purely psychological. If we destroy it, our brains may resort back to thinking they need to keep track of the tasks.

As uncomfortable as it can be, we need to be OK with letting these non-essential items fall by the wayside. If we get to them, great! But if not, we know it's not going to be the end of the world.

We will be Time-Blocking only the essential tasks we pick out from the list and keeping those things front and center. With this simple discipline, Time-Blocking helps us remain focused.

PICK THREE

When we approach Time-Blocking our day (also known as "Day-Blocking"), it's crucial to determine our essentials for *today*. While we may have determined several tasks we deem important, we must also figure out which of those are necessary for us to complete today only.

I'm going to suggest you do something a bit radical: Pick only three.

Several years ago, I heard a podcast by best-selling author and brand consultant, Donald Miller. In this particular episode, he described his process for planning out his day. The thing he said that intrigued me the most was that he only allows himself to choose three primary projects to work on for any given day.

Miller stated that by picking just three things, it sets up a safeguard for completing his most meaningful work for that day. He knows, if he allows himself to work on seven or eight miscellaneous tasks but doesn't get something done to advance his goals, he will consider that day a failure. That's why he recommends picking just three.

I have since begun applying this to my daily work. It has been a game-changer for me, and it just so happens to compliment the Time-Blocking methodology very well.

Why only three tasks? Well, you have to admit that there is something special—even sacred—about this number (the three dimensions, the Holy Trinity, and the Three Stooges). But aside from this, one of the biggest reasons why we must limit our daily tasks is because of "The Planning Fallacy." This concept, conceived by two psychologists, Daniel Kahneman and Amos Tversky, in the 1970s, basically states that people are prone to overestimate the time it will take to complete a task, even if they have performed the task before.

To illustrate how drastic this bias can be, students working on their final thesis at the University of Waterloo (in Ontario, Canada) were asked to estimate the amount of time they thought it would take to complete their papers. The average response was around thirty-four days. Now, keep in mind, these students had written similar papers before, so they knew full well everything it would take to complete them. Yet, when the final projects were turned in, the average completion time ended up being fifty-five days. The students had been off by an entire three weeks![viii]

When we begin planning our tasks for the day, the week, and the year, we must recognize our tendency to be overly optimistic. Donald Miller admits that many days, he does not even get to all three of his tasks. This tells me that focusing on only three things per day is not aiming too low; it is just about right, and in some cases, it might be aiming too high.

I can attest to this. On the days I think, "Oh, I can still squeeze in this fourth thing," I almost never get to it. So, I challenge you to only pick three essential tasks for any given day.

To give you a specific example, my three things for today are:

1. Write for one hour on this book.
2. Onboard my new social media manager.
3. Edit a video.

You can think of these three things as three goals or three outcomes for the day. The point is not necessarily to choose three tasks that are only going to take fifteen minutes each. If you do have several smaller tasks like this, you should see how you can batch them into one overarching goal so that you can Time-Block that goal.

You'll notice that some of the tasks I mentioned above are going to involve subtasks. Onboarding a new contractor will involve me writing out instructions for them, providing necessary login information, and sending them a contractor's agreement. And even for the task of editing a video, there are a few different steps. First, I'll be choosing the best clips of the video and color grading in Premiere Pro. Then second, I'll be using an online app to add captions to the video.

The other reason why you need to choose only three tasks brings us back to the concept of *focus*. When we can dedicate our workday to extreme focus on just three things, we are able to achieve more by doing less. And this is the next rule:

Rule #3 of Time-Blocking is to *achieve more by doing less*.

Focusing on fewer things in the day can go against the very fabric of our being, but it is crucial. Whether you believe me or not, it will empower you to do *more*. And if you are faithful in applying your essentials to these three things, it will allow you to achieve *better* outcomes.

By doing less—adding fewer tasks to our day—we reduce the toll of task-switching.

The first way we reduce the amount of task-switching in our day we've already discussed: stop multitasking. Remember, what we think is multitasking is actually just rapid task-switching from one thing to the next. This excessive amount of task-switching is harmful to our productivity.

But even if we were to completely remove multitasking from the conversation, we would find that we still do a lot of task-switching throughout our day—more than we realize. So, the second way we can reduce task-switching further is simply by doing less. Less activities mean less task-switching. By choosing just three essential tasks for our workday, we're able to not only give our focus to those three things, but also reduce the number of times we have to shift our focus.

Focus is not a limitless resource. Remember, it is something that needs to be managed.

Let's say we assigned a dollar value to our focus. We could say that each time we focused on a task, uninterrupted for any span of time, it costs us $1.00. We'll call these "focus bucks."

Our goal should be to spend as little focus bucks as we can throughout our day.

Let's say we are writing an important email, and in the middle of that, our phone pings a notification telling us someone has commented on our social media post. So, we go check out the comment before returning to the email. Many of us do this sort of thing all the time, and while it may seem that we've only lost a few seconds of time, we are also spending focus bucks.

Two tasks, which should have otherwise cost $2.00 total, now cost $3.00 because we had to switch back and forth between these things. Spending one extra buck here may seem insignificant, but let's say you get pinged not once but three times over the course of writing that email. Now, you've spent $7.00:

- $1.00 – Starting the email
- $1.00 – Notification, checking social media
- $1.00 – Back to the email, rereading what you last wrote, and picking up where you left off
- $1.00 – Checking social media
- $1.00 – Back to the email
- $1.00 – Checking social media
- $1.00 – Back to the email and finally finishing

By task-switching, we've spent more than triple the amount of focus energy than if we had just maintained single-focus on two tasks separately.

What the above analogy doesn't take into account is that focus, like energy, gets depleted over time. With rest and a good night's sleep, it can be replenished at the beginning of each day, but as the day goes on, we have less and less of it.

So, in reality, our focus bucks accrue interest with every task we add to our day. For our purposes, let's say that every new task adds an additional $.25 because we have to use more brain power to focus on that task. Here's an example of what my day could look like if I tried getting six different things done:

- $1.00 – Task #1
- $1.25 – Task #2
- $1.50 – Task #3
- $2.00 – Task #4
- $2.25 – Task #5
- $2.50 – Task #6

Total = $10.50

Compare this to the total of $3.75, which I would have used by only focusing on three tasks.

In most cases, we wouldn't actually get to all six of these tasks in a day. And at the very least, we would get very little work done on each thing or do a sub-par job on each task. Something is going to suffer because you'll notice that, by the time we arrive at the fourth task, we are having to use double the amount of focus energy as we did for Task #1.

But by reducing our daily tasks and goals to three, we are able to significantly preserve our mental energy to give adequate focus to our three essentials.

WIN YOUR DAY

We also can't neglect the fact that our ability to focus on a task is often tied to whether or not we are motivated to do it.

When we fail to complete a project in the time we planned, this can be demotivating. We feel unproductive and blame ourselves for not working fast enough or hard enough. But we've simply fallen victim to the Planning Fallacy.

By contrast, on those days when we check off all of the things on our To-Do list, we feel extremely productive. This fuels our drives to get even more done. As we've discussed, this can be harmful if we are simply getting non-essential things done. But by working on our essentials, we can use this productivity high to our advantage.

One of our goals in Time-Blocking will be to achieve small wins. These small wins translate into big wins because they motivate us to keep moving forward toward our larger goals. To do this, we have to set ourselves up for success. We must set realistic goals for our day and not fall prey to the Planning Fallacy.

By picking three essential tasks every day, you can do this!

Aiming for just three outcomes is not aiming too low. It's shooting for the stars. We are taking a few small steps toward achieving our biggest dreams and not wasting our focus on excess tasks. We can achieve more by doing less!

Focus is a limited resource, however there is a way that we can make some of it back throughout the day. That is what Rule #4 is all about . . .

CHAPTER FOUR

PLAN TO RECHARGE

In order to be successful with the Time-Blocking Method, there are a few things we will be intentionally blocking in our schedule. Our Three Essential Tasks is the first.

The second is equally important but something many of us resist: rest.

NO MORE RECESS

In early elementary school, my school gave us three recess periods throughout the day. It's every kid's favorite subject, right? Recess was for kickball, tag, and playing on the jungle gym. It was a time to unwind between taking spelling tests and learning times tables.

But when I reached the third grade, something quite traumatic happened. I walked into my first day of school and learned, to my dismay, we'd only be getting *one* recess. "That's not fair!" thought my eight-year-old self.

Fast forward a few years later to junior high, and they eliminated recess entirely from the school day. This seemed to be the reality of growing up: more work, less play.

What I was subtly being taught was that taking breaks is *bad*. Stopping and taking time away from work was lazy. The need for rest came to be perceived as a form of weakness.

Due to such social pressures (and even pressure from ourselves), we work long hours. Sometimes, we work through lunch. We even work on the weekend (a practice especially common among entrepreneurs).

We believe that taking breaks is something only children need. But this could be no further from the truth. It's very likely we need breaks even more often as adults.

The problem is, even if we take the socially prescribed rest of a one-hour lunch break and two days off on the weekend, it's not enough. We need frequent breaks every day, possibly every hour.

LAZY, OR SMART?

While Time-Blocking as a practice can be traced as far back as the 1700s with Benjamin Franklin,[ix] the earliest systemized version of Time-Blocking is known as the Pomodoro Technique. It was developed in the 1980s by Italian philosopher Francesco Cirillo. He would practice twenty-five-minute sprints (or Time-Blocks) of focused work, and between each sprint, he would take a five-minute break. Then, after repeating this process four consecutive times, he would take a longer break.

Though I'm not convinced that twenty-five minutes should be the prescribed amount of time for everyone, I do think there is a lot we can learn from Cirillo's methodology—the most important being that he built in rest as a daily practice.

In order to be successful in Time-Blocking, we must do the same. This is part of managing our focus, which is tied to our energy levels. To have the fullest amount of focus and be our most productive selves, we must *plan to recharge.*

Rule #4 of Time-Blocking is to *plan to recharge.*

I will let you know right now: This is going to be an uphill battle for many of you reading this. We already have the social pressures looming over us, telling us to work harder. Work more. Take less breaks.

But for many of us (myself included), the even stronger pressure comes from within. We want to prove to ourselves that we're not lazy. We hate failure and don't want others to perceive us as failures. So, we hustle and do everything we deem necessary to succeed, even if that means all work and no play.

It is time to tear through these lies, and replace them with the truth: We will actually be more productive when we rest and recharge.

In a study published by DeskTime, they analyzed the top ten percent most productive employees using their time tracking software. What they discovered was that the most productive employees were the ones who took the most frequent breaks. On average, these individuals would work for fifty-two minutes then take a seventeen-minute break, repeating this pattern throughout the workday.[x]

This seems counterintuitive, doesn't it?

I can imagine their coworkers must have thought *they* were the lazy ones–slacking off and not taking their work seriously.

"Why do they take so many *unnecessary* breaks while the rest of us are working our butts off the entire day?"

But this ten percent was not lazy. They simply understood that resting allowed them to *work smarter*.

So how do breaks make you more productive? Why is it that you can get more done by working less? There are a few reasons for this:

If you are sitting at a desk all day, you may not think you are exerting much energy, but in fact, you are working one of the most important muscles in your body: your brain. And guess which muscle is responsible for your focus. That's right, your brain. Your mind requires rest just like your body does after a hard workout. This is, of course, the reason we need sleep. Sleep allows our brains to recharge after a full day of constant activity.

But as we are trying to achieve more focused work, we find that our brain needs more than just sleep every night to stay engaged throughout the day. Most of today's work requires a lot of concentration, and that "focus energy" slowly gets depleted due to those hours of intense labor.

When we don't rest our minds frequently, our productivity gradually suffers as the day goes on. And halfway through the day, we find ourselves running on fumes, relying on sheer will-power to get things done. But will-power without the ability to focus is virtually useless. We may still be working hard, but our hard work is not yielding the optimal results.

I'm sure you've been there before. It's two 'o clock in the afternoon, and you feel "the slump" set in. Your mind starts to fog up, and you feel like taking a nap. Our bodies are communicating to us that it's time for a break. But what do we do? We grab some coffee and power through. While this may give us a quick jumpstart to keep going, our productivity is on "E" and will continue declining.

Resting our brain simply means focusing on something different, something that doesn't require nearly as much concentration. Watch a funny cat video, converse with your coworkers, or go for a walk. These are just a few ideas.

PRESS RESET

Another reason why our productivity suffers by not taking breaks is due to a phenomenon called "vigilance decrement." Studies have shown that focusing for too long on any given task hinders your performance of that task.

University of Illinois professor Alejandro Lleras says this is because our brain tends to register constant stimulation as unimportant. For example, if you were to put on a hat before leaving the house, you may initially notice the feeling of the material against your scalp, but it is not long before you no longer notice it. Your awareness that you are even wearing the hat practically disappears for the majority of time wearing it.

Can you imagine your brain having to think, "I'm wearing a hat, I'm wearing a hat," all day long? It would use up all of its energy on such a menial activity. But with the amazing design that our brains have, it doesn't do this. It stops registering it so that you're ready to react to and focus on new stimuli.

Lleras says the same thing happens when you work on a task for too long, especially on one that is more repetitive. Your brain eventually registers this consistent activity as less important, decreasing your awareness of it, and that is why your focus begins to decline.

The simple fix for this is to take a break. This acts as a reset button for your brain. Lleras suggested that by deactivating and reactivating your goals, you're able to maintain better focus on your task.

SCHEDULE TIMES OF REST

As I said, for many of us, this will be an uphill battle. Our natural tendency will be to keep working, even when our body is telling us to do otherwise. And we may not even notice as our focus wanes due to vigilance decrement from doing the same task for too long. We need to take our rest seriously and be intentional about it.

Fortunately, Time-Blocking offers the very framework we need to plan times of rest! In Part 2 of this book, when we begin to design our day, we will schedule purposeful times to take breaks. Now, the exact times we choose to take breaks will vary quite a bit from person to person, but the frequency with which we take them should not.

So *how often* should we schedule breaks, and *how long* should they be?

The Pomodoro Technique prescribes one five-minute break every twenty-five minutes. The DeskTime study seemed to show seventeen-minute breaks after fifty-two-minute sprints to be optimal. Robert C. Pozen in *Extreme Productivity: Boost Your Results, Reduce Your Hours* recommends working no longer than seventy-five to ninety minutes at a time, based on the practice regimen of most professional musicians. And still, other publications have suggested taking a break every sixty to ninety minutes.

The answer? It depends.

First of all, we are all different. We all work at different paces and have different attention spans. I have come across many individuals who say that taking a break every twenty-five minutes is perfect for them. For me, however, I have found that while writing a book (for instance), it takes me close to twenty minutes to get fully in the zone. To quit after only twenty-five minutes would actually interrupt my creative flow and be more harmful to my productivity.

So, it depends on the task being performed. Some work is going to require more concentration than others, resulting in varied amounts of time required to focus in on a task as well as time required to rest after that task.

However, one thing that is consistent is that we need to think about this less in terms of *how many breaks we should take per day*. In his book, Pozen says, "The real question is what is the appropriate time period of concentrated work you can do before taking break?"

We can safely say that the sweet spot is somewhere in the sixty- to ninety-minute range. And when you take your break, it should last at least five minutes. Closer to fifteen minutes is even better. Then, after about three to four hours of work, you should also take a longer break of thirty minutes to an hour.

These numbers can be your starting place. What we will do in Section 2 as part of implementing the Time-Blocking method is test what is going to be best for you. Your (1) "Three Things" and your (2) breaks will be the two most important things to Time-Block each day.

We've already discussed the obstacle of societal pressure, which prevents us from taking the breaks we need. However, this is not the only outside force keeping us from achieving productive work. We'll address this in our fifth and final Rule of Time-Blocking.

CHAPTER FIVE

TAKE BACK CONTROL OF YOUR TIME

Everyone's got their own agenda.

Your boss has an agenda. Your coworker has an agenda. Your spouse has an agenda. Your mom. Your in-laws. Your best friend. Your pastor. Your coach. Your therapist. Your employee. Your client. And you—you have your own agenda, too.

Everyone is approaching their life, their work, their relationships, everything from a different angle. They have different values, different priorities, and different goals. And there's nothing wrong with that.

It is extremely important for you to recognize this. And by the very nature of this fact, you must also be aware that not everyone has an agenda that is going to align with your agenda. Again, nothing wrong with that.

For any of us to accomplish whatever it is we are trying to accomplish, it often requires imposing our agendas on another person. As poet John Donne reminds us, "No man is an island." We cannot accomplish anything of significance alone. We need each other.

When two people come together whose agendas align with each other, collaboration is able to happen. There is harmony.

But this is not always the case. In fact, the majority of the time, the goals of the two individuals will differ and, in other cases, be polar opposites. The clashing of these separate agendas can lead to mutual compromise or conflict. That would be the best case scenario. Yes, you heard me right. Even conflict would be a better result than the third option: passivity.

This reaction lies somewhere in the middle, and, in reality, it's not a reaction at all. It's inaction. This is the default. Inaction is still a choice (conscious or not) to go with the flow and let your life be dictated by someone else's agenda.

In an extreme case of this, you can be passive to the point of becoming a doormat, letting others walk all over you. You never voice your opinion, never stick up for yourself, and as a result, rarely get what you want. I hope that we can all agree that this is an unhealthy way to approach life.

However, even if you don't struggle with being a doormat, there is a more subtle way that we become passive in our lives, and it affects more than we realize. It's with our time.

Most of us approach time in a passive way, without a clear gameplan. We've previously talked about articulating our goals and determining what our focus should be. You would think that simply knowing these things and working toward them would be enough. It would be, if it weren't for other people's agendas.

When we take a passive approach to our schedule, we leave the door open for someone else to determine it for us.

We've all been there before. You're knee-deep, focused on that important project, when all of a sudden your phone rings. You thought it was an important call, but it ended up just being a telemarketer. Or your coworker walks over to your cubicle to tell you about their weekend. Or you open an email from a disgruntled customer who claims to need your assistance right now.

These are individuals imposing their agendas on you. At best, they become a momentary distraction, causing a lapse in your focus. At worst, you end up conceding and address their wants and needs, even when it does not align with your goals in that moment.

It would be easy to get angry and blame these other people for "trying" to keep us from accomplishing our goals, but that just wouldn't be fair. For one thing, their reason for interrupting us may be entirely legitimate: that pesky telemarketer is merely doing their job. Your coworker wants to build a friendship with you. That upset customer really does need your help.

We, ourselves, make requests of others, too. We rely on other people all the time. This is part of life.

The real responsibility lies on our shoulders; if we don't intentionally take control of our time, others will gladly step in to do it for us. This is the next rule:

Time-Blocking Rule #5 is to *take back control of your time*.

You deserve to make this promise to yourself, so you can be the most productive with Time-Blocking. Say it out loud. Write it on a sticky note for you to see every day if you have to: "I hereby commit to take back control of my time and not let others dictate my schedule."

There are a few things you can do to keep this promise to yourself.

THE DIRTY WORD

In an effort to gain other people's approval, "yes" becomes our default response.

Yes, of course, is a wonderful word to hear. A *yes* to a dinner date. A *yes* to a raise. A *yes* from a potential client.

By contrast, "no" is often viewed as negative. As rejection. For all of the people-pleasers out there, it can feel like a dirty word.

But "no" is not a four-letter word. In fact, it can be a very empowering word.

Can you remember a moment when you said "yes" to something, and later regretted it? In that moment, did you feel empowered? Probably not. You probably felt *stuck*. You committed to something you wish you hadn't, and now you feel like you will lose out on precious time. This new obligation may have even prevented you from doing something else important with that time.

Hindsight is always 20/20. After the fact, you probably even wished you had said, "No." But that's easy to say after the fact. In the moment, saying "no" is often the more uncomfortable option, even though it would've made you happier in the long run. You defaulted to yes.

I want to challenge the way you think about these words: Yes does not mean yes. Yes means no.

Confused? I know, it doesn't seem to make sense. But if you think about it, saying "yes" actually carries more rejection than saying "no."

Recall for a moment the last wedding ceremony you attended. When the bride and groom met each other at the altar and uttered the words, "I do," think about what that meant. We often think of it in terms of, "Yes, I choose to marry you." But this is only half true.

With that final, "I do," they also said a big fat "No" to everyone else! This one yes is a huge rejection to the other seven billion people in the world.

Yes is always a package deal that also comes with several *nos*. Any time you say yes to something, you are automatically saying no to the many alternatives.

This inverse is also true. No also does not just mean *no*. *No* means *yes*. By saying no to one thing that you deem as less important, you free yourself to answer, "Yes" to important things. There is freedom in the word no.

You deserve it to yourself to make "no" a part of your regular vocabulary.

Your family and those closest to you also deserve it. A "no" to your boss requesting that you work late may mean a yes to having dinner at the table with your family. A "no" to your chatty co-worker may mean getting your work done early enough to attend your child's sports meet or recital. A "no" to work on the weekend may allow you to catch up with a friend.

When it comes to Time-Blocking, saying "no" to a person or opportunity is often saying "yes" to yourself. And this is not in a selfish way. The word no allows you to take back control of your own schedule.

APPOINTMENTS WITH YOURSELF

In Section 2 of this book, we will set up our Time-Blocks for focused time on a task or activity. But when we do this, we must also learn to guard our Time-Blocks unapologetically.

Our Time-Blocks have the potential to provide us with many benefits to our lives but only if we hail them as sacred. That's because distractions and interruptions *will* occur. We have to stand strong in our commitment to make our Time-Blocks as productive as possible.

You see, your Time-Blocks are appointments that you make with yourself.

I can almost guarantee that if you set an appointment on the calendar—whether that be a business meeting, a dentist appointment, or something else—you are going to do everything in your power to make that appointment. We prioritize these sorts of daily events, but we somehow treat other essential tasks more loosely. *We'll get to it when we can.*

But if our essentials are truly as such, don't you think we should pencil them in the same way we do our other appointments?

When you have an important project that you planned to work on all afternoon, and someone wants to schedule a phone call last minute, you can tell them, "I'm sorry, but I have an appointment scheduled for this time. Can we schedule this for a different time?" I can't imagine anyone having an objection to that. Viewing your Time-Blocks in this way will help you guard them better.

But be warned because you will be tested. Trust me, as soon as you commit to making Time-Blocking a regular practice, people will come out of the woodwork to impose their own agendas on you. It will seem as if the universe has suddenly conspired against you to keep you from your Time-Blocks. You must be ready. You need to have the resolve, as well as the tools in place, to stay committed to your goals.

Now, what if something comes up? What do you do when something must be addressed immediately? What if it is an emergency?

In many cases—I would dare say, in *most* cases—this is the wrong question to ask. What you should be questioning is, *Is this really an emergency?*

There is a good chance that you are in the habit of being interrupted by false alarms. When well-meaning individuals approach you in an urgent or frantic manor, it is easy to be tricked into thinking that their agenda is truly an emergency. This false sense of urgency is very counterproductive to your goals, and we need to nip it in the bud.

We need to have a quick way to qualify these so-called "emergencies," so we can either respond to true ones or ignore them and continue with our important tasks at hand. Instead of simply agreeing with the other person that *this must be done now*, ask yourself the critical question: *What would happen if I didn't do this now?*

What would be the consequence? Certainly, there are consequences to any action, whether positive or negative. The question is, would the repercussions be major or minor?

For example, let's say that you are in the middle of an important task, which you have previously Time-Blocked. In the middle of this, a client asks you to make revisions to a project, and they state they need it done today. Ask yourself, what would happen if you told them you couldn't, that the soonest you would be able to get to it was tomorrow? Would you lose them as a client? Would their business completely fail? Or would they simply be temporarily inconvenienced and quickly come to accept they will just have to wait another day?

In my experience, few things are actually as urgent as people may lead you to think, and if you always concede these outside agendas, you will never accomplish your own goals. Again, saying "no," or simply "later" is not wrong. It is actually healthy.

Remember, saying "yes" unquestioningly is living life by default. Only when you take a moment to think critically about these outside agendas and are willing to say "no" when necessary, can you start approaching your work and your life with intention.

And by doing so, the ones who tend to push their "urgent" agendas on you the most will begin to learn better boundaries with you. They may not like it at first, but in time, they will come to respect you for it.

TOO MUCH COMMUNICATION

You now should have a better idea of how to handle those requests that tend to eat up your time when they come (and they will). But as you might imagine, having to say "no" all the time can get exhausting. So, there is one more safeguard we can put into place, which will actually help limit the amount of conflicting agendas we must deal with on a daily basis: We have to Time-Block our communication.

At the end of the day, it is our fault when we let others take control of our schedule, and that is because we give them too many opportunities to do so. Good communication is clearly important, but I fear that in a world that is so connected as ours, we may be allowing too much communication. Between messaging apps, email, social media, phone calls, video conferences, and beyond, we not only have more access to the world than we ever have in history, but the world also has more access to us.

When someone can reach us at any moment of any day, it means that we have the potential to be interrupted at any moment of any day. As we've discussed before, when these interruptions occur, we temporarily lose focus, and it takes time and mental energy to recover from these shifts in focus. Multiply this by the countless emails, texts, and calls we receive throughout the day, it's a wonder how we get anything done at all.

The solution is we must limit the amount of time we spend on activities that involve communication. What holds many of us back from doing this is the concern that it will result in major breakdowns in communication, but it actually lends itself to more efficient communication.

Have you ever come out of an hour-long meeting with the feeling that the same information could have been shared in half the time? You were probably right. Unfortunately, this is an example of how the time we allot for communication (in this case, a meeting) is time that we find ways to fill up unnecessarily. We discuss something for an hour only because we have an hour to talk about it.

And the reality is, if we each began to limit the amount of time we spend communicating, we likely would not see any major decline in our quality of communication. We would have more time to actually act on what was discussed.

We can go about limiting our communication in this way with Time-Blocking, setting aside specific segments of the day for it. In *The 4-Hour Work Week*, Tim Ferriss addresses this issue when it comes to checking email. Rather than frequenting the inbox throughout the day, like many of us tend to do, he recommends blocking off no more than two times per day to check and respond to emails.

He suggests doing this right before lunch and at the very end of the day.[xi] You should determine the best times based on your own schedule, but I can tell you that these specific times have worked very well for me. Ferriss rationalizes that by waiting to check emails until later in the day—once before a major break, and once before quitting time—you are able to focus on your most important tasks during your most productive times of the day.

The problem when you check your email first thing in the morning is that you are opening the floodgates for those outside requests to start coming in. Regardless of what you had planned to do that morning, now you have become bombarded by more to-dos. Even if you decide to not address those to-dos then and go back to your original plan, you now have these issues lingering in the back of your mind.

The purpose, Ferriss says, is to resist checking emails at times when you are not prepared to address them. If you check an email which you don't plan to respond to until later, you have just wasted precious minutes and put an unnecessary weight on your shoulders that will divide your focus for the rest of the day. For this same reason, Ferriss also recommends not checking email in the evening when you are "off the clock," since you are not in a position to put out any fires until the next morning anyway. This could unnecessarily preoccupy you with work-related worries at a time when you are supposed to be unwinding.

I concur with Ferriss and believe this principle applies to any form of unplanned communication. That includes phone calls, Slack messages, social media comments, etc. We can maximize our time and better manage our focus when we design specific Time-Blocks to focus on these forms of communication that tend to involve other people imposing their agendas on us.

Again, you have to apply this to your own unique situation. If your work requires you to do a lot of customer service or outbound calling/emailing, you will obviously have to deal with these forms of communication throughout the day. But the principle still applies. It is the reason I use the term "unplanned communication"—even for you, you'll want to limit your use of other communication channels that do not relate to your current Time-Blocked activity.

For example, let's say you need to spend time cold-calling for your business. This is a task you have been putting off for weeks, but you finally decide to set aside a span of time to call a list of leads. In other words, you have Time-Blocked this task. That's great! But then, let's say during this Time-Block, you get a phone call from an existing client. Do you answer?

In short, no! This time was set aside for one thing: cold calling. Answering that phone call would likely mean an unexpected conversation for an undetermined amount of time, and you would most likely receive a new request.

I can already hear the objections from a few of you reading this. I know there are those of you who would have a difficult time leaving that call unanswered. But you know what, that's why they invented voicemail.

My wife would admit that she really struggles with this. Her first instinct is to respond to any call, text, or email immediately. To her credit, her intentions are pure, as she strives to be helpful and give a timely response. I applaud the heart behind this; however, I have come to learn that it is unrealistic, especially when productivity is the goal. And there is no rule that says that you have to respond to anything right away. Remember, very few things are truly an emergency.

For the person on the other end of the phone call, for all they know, you are driving down the freeway, at the doctor's office, or in another appointment . . . and you are! Remember, your Time-Block is an appointment you made with yourself. Answering that phone call would only enable you to continue procrastinating on that important task.

If you find yourself in a similar scenario, I challenge you to let it go to voicemail, wait until you have spare time to listen to it, then call them back as soon as possible. Most people will understand and think nothing of it!

The way we can finally take back control of our time is to set limits, and often, it involves saying "no." It may mean saying "no" to requests that come our way that don't align with our objectives. It may mean saying "no" to doing certain activities, such as checking email all day long. But a "no" to these things, will mean saying "yes" to accomplishing our goals.

So, you've now learned the Five Rules of Time-Blocking which make up the Time-Blocking Mindset. Before we move on, let's quickly revisit them:

1. Maintain Single-Focus (a.k.a. Stop Multitasking)
2. Determine Your Essentials (a.k.a. Reverse Engineer Your Goals)
3. Achieve More by Doing Less (a.k.a. Pick Three Things)
4. Plan to Recharge (a.k.a. Schedule Times of Rest)
5. Take Back Control of Your Time (a.k.a. Learn to Say "No")

If you follow these five guidelines, you will begin to see boosts in your productivity. Now that we have the tools we need, it's time to apply these principles in a framework known as the Time-Blocking Method.

SECTION II

the

TIME-BLOCKING METHOD

CHAPTER SIX

MACRO-BLOCKING

The Time-Blocking Method has three different applications. You may choose to apply just one or two of them, and that is totally fine. But they work best when applied in conjunction with each other.

The three different forms of Time-Blocking are:

1. Macro-Blocking
2. Micro-Blocking
3. Day-Blocking

We will start with Macro-Blocking because, as the name suggests, it will allow us to approach productivity on the macro level.

This section of the book will provide you with practical steps that you can start implementing immediately. I encourage you to complete any action steps as we go along, so be prepared to write some things down!

And to make it as easy as possible, I have provided space in the first section of The Time-Blocking Day Planner for you to answer these questions. If you haven't yet picked up a copy, be sure to visit timeblockingbook.com to order your planner.

Let's begin!

MACRO-LEVEL FOCUS

Macro-Blocking is the form of Time-Blocking where we designate larger segments of time to a single focus. These spans of time can be anywhere from a few days to an entire year. Unlike the other two forms of Time-Blocking, where we zero-in on specific tasks, this form allows us to focus on large goals and outcomes.

I didn't realize it at the time, but I had been applying Macro-Blocking in my business long before I had heard the term Time-Blocking.

My company, One Nine Pro, is a branding and marketing agency. We primarily help businesses establish their brand, starting with brand strategy, and design their brand identity (or aesthetics), as well as develop brand messaging. We also create marketing materials, including websites, which apply these brand elements.

By the very nature of it, this is a one-off service, which does not require much ongoing maintenance. Others who offer similar services tend to work with multiple clients and multiple projects at a time. And this is the way I was approaching it as well.

But then I came across another graphic designer who was doing things a bit differently. Lauren Hooker, founder of Elle & Company, shared in her webinar the way she approached working with clients, which was vastly different from what most designers were doing at the time. She opted for working with one client at a time. And she did so for a set period, conferring with the client to determine the dates they would work together. During this span of time, she would treat them as if they were her only client. And once those weeks were over, she would do the same for the next client booked on the calendar.

A lightbulb went off in my head. The benefits of working this way became so clear to me when I heard it that I applied it to my business immediately.

Remember how we discussed the dangers of multitasking? I had previously been multitasking with my branding projects, trying to juggle several clients at a time. But this new process allowed me to practice single-focus. I could provide dedicated time and attention to my client, and by doing so, provide a better, faster result. It allowed me to work with a much clearer mind, focusing on the objective at hand and avoiding the stress that comes with juggling multiple unrelated projects. I began booking my client projects in advance and blocking off specific weeks on my calendar to work with them. It has worked very well for me since then.

This is a great example of Macro-Blocking. Dedicating single-focus to a larger objective for a set period of time can give you the clarity of thought to reach a goal faster.

To be clear, it is not saying you will only work on just one task for weeks on end. For most of us, that would be unrealistic. We all have many other responsibilities to attend to, and so the point of this is not to neglect the rest of your tasks. Rather Macro-Blocking is about committing your overall focus on a single goal.

However, with that said, it should affect your schedule in some way. If you are committing to focusing on this goal, what needs to change? What measures do you need to put in place during this Macro-Block of time? Do you need to block off the same hours every day to work on it? Do you need to cut out any previous obligations or social activities? Do you need to change up your work environment by getting out in nature or going to a library to get in the right frame of mind?

While writing this book, I decided to Macro-Block several weeks for the goal of completing my first draft. During which, I continued to run my business and attend to my other responsibilities, but with my manuscript being the main focus of these weeks, I did make drastic changes to my routine, setting aside half of my workday just for writing.

REVERSE ENGINEER YOUR ESSENTIALS

In Chapter 2, I challenged you to consider your essentials. Now, it is time to turn those essentials into actionable steps. If Macro-Blocking can help us reach larger, long-term goals, then we need to look to our essentials to determine exactly what we should Time-Block on the macro-level.

In your *Time-Blocking Day Planner*, you may refer to Section 1 entitled, "Determine Your Essentials." Here we are going to list out several things.

YOUR PURPOSE STATEMENT

First, I feel it is important to start by writing out your Purpose Statement. Again, you can think of this as your life's mission statement or your "why."

> **MY PURPOSE STATEMENT:**
>
> To use my gift of creativity to empower the poor.
>
> **MY VALUES:**
>
> - Date nights with my spouse
> - Never missing my kid's sporting event
> - Caring for my elderly parent
> - Debt freedom
> - Success in business
> -

If you have never written this out or even considered this before reading this book, now is the perfect time!

What drives you? What gets you up in the morning? What are you called to do? Try your best to boil it down to one or two sentences.

Here is mine: *To use my gift of creativity to empower the poor.*

I believe this to be my purpose in life, and it is very specific to me and what drives me.

YOUR VALUES

Below this, create a list of your values. Be as specific as you can about the things you value most. Some examples might be:

- Date nights with my spouse
- Never missing my kid's sporting event
- Caring for my elderly parent
- Debt freedom
- Success in business
- Supporting veterans
- Volunteering with local charities

You may be tempted to skip these first two steps and move on to what many will deem the more "practical" steps, but please take these steps seriously. It is so easy for any of us to be distracted and lose sight of what is most important. This exercise will be vital to your productivity journey because it is our values that translate into our goals. If we don't create goals with our true values in mind, we may find that we have gotten a lot of stuff done, yet we are unfulfilled.

LIFE GOALS

So, with these values in mind, let us list out as many of our life goals that we can think of. Life goals can encompass anything that you may wish to accomplish this year or forty years from now. In this section, there are no wrong answers. Even the most outrageous goals are fair game here. So, feel free to take a moment to dream big!

To give you some ideas, here are a few of mine:

- Have the means to travel and live abroad in exotic locations with my family
- Own more than five rental properties

- Donate or raise more than one million dollars to empower the poor
- Pay off student loans
- Become a best-selling author

For the realists out there (of which, I am one), don't worry: in the next section, we will narrow these down even further.

THIS YEAR'S GOALS

Perhaps you have started to pick up on what we are doing here. This is the process of reverse engineering our essentials. We started at the ten-thousand-foot view by listing our purpose statement, went a level deeper by looking at our values, and then let those values reveal our life goals. And now, it is time to choose our goals for this year.

Look at your list of Life Goals. Which of these do you want to tackle this year? Write them down as a separate list. For those using *The Time-Blocking Day Planner*, you can write these on the section designated for This Year's Goals.

Reminding us again of our goal-setting guidelines, your goals for this year should be:

1. Specific
2. Measurable
3. Actionable
4. Realistic
5. Time-Bound

Double check to make sure your goals fit this criteria.

Now, as you begin to evaluate whether or not your goals are realistic, what you will likely notice is that some of your larger goals may not be realistic for completing this year. Often, achieving our biggest dreams takes longer than just one year.

So, what I want you to do is take that larger Life Goal and write out the possible steps toward achieving the goal over the next several years. Then, choose one goal you can make for this year that would push the needle forward on your larger goal.

For example, let's say that one of your Life Goals is to become one of the leading authorities on the topic of emotional intelligence. This is obviously a huge goal and one that, realistically, you probably would not be able to achieve in a single year. But there are certain sub-goals you could set for yourself that would allow you to keep moving toward that goal. Some examples could be to write a book on emotional intelligence, create an online course or training, film a video series, or book speaking engagements. When you start to break down this seemingly impossible goal into smaller, actionable goals, they start to seem not so crazy after all!

The problem, when we set such high goals, is not that we have set our sights too high, but simply that we stop there. You see, big goals are often too abstract, making it impossible to take action on them. I am actually a big proponent of setting audacious goals, but those audacious goals must eventually translate into real plans. That is why we must reverse engineer our goals into smaller ones; they'll empower us to make moves.

In my experience, there are often two types of personalities when it comes to goal-setting: Big Dreamers and Small Dreamers. As the name implies, Big Dreamers dream big. This personality type tends to have a more futuristic mindset and sets more audacious goals. Small Dreamers are better at focusing on the here-and-now and are more conservative in their goal setting because they are more realistic. There is nothing wrong with either of these approaches, but I think it is important to understand the limitations that tend to come with each.

If you are a Big Dreamer, I want you to look at your list of This Year's Goals and subtract one goal from the list. This is because those with this personality are more prone to overestimate what they can achieve. This is not to stifle you from reaching for the stars but to set you up for success. Setting goals that end up being unattainable can be discouraging and demotivating when you end up failing to achieve them. Even by crossing off one goal from your list, I would wager you are still shooting high with what you are looking to achieve.

I tend to fall more into the Small Dreamer camp. If this is you, I am going to challenge you to do the opposite. In an effort to be "more realistic" with your goals, there is a good chance you are not pushing yourself enough out of your comfort zone with your goal-setting. So, I challenge you to add one more big goal to your list for this year.

If you haven't already at this point, I want to challenge you to include in one or two goals related to rest and pouring back into yourself. This is in line with our Time-Blocking Rule #4: plan to recharge. Such goals could include taking a family vacation to Disney World or taking a monthly camping trip. These goals should not be neglected or undervalued since, as we've discussed, taking extended times to recharge will only improve your productivity in the long run, not take away from it.

> ○ Own 5+ rental properties   ○
> ○ Become a best-selling author   ○
> ○   ○
>
>
> **This Year's Goals**
>
> ○ Create an online course   ○ Build my persona
> ○ Speak on 20 podcasts   ★ Grow startup
> ○ Take 3 vacations   ○
> ★ Buy one investment property ○
> ○ Raise $25k for charity   ○
> ★ Write my novel   ○

TOP THREE ESSENTIAL GOALS

The last thing I want you to do with your goals for this year is to pick your top three. Decide the three that are most essential to you, and put a star next to them. At this stage, I am not telling you to shorten your list of This Year's Goals any more. This exercise will simply allow you to prioritize even the *most essential* of your essential goals.

Ask yourself, "If I were to come to the end of this year having accomplished only three outcomes, what would I want those to be?"

TIME-BLOCK YOUR GOALS

Now that we've determined our goals for this year, the final step is to Macro-Block these goals, starting with the top three. If these three outcomes are the ones you absolutely must achieve before the end of the year, it makes sense to block them first.

Next to each of those goals on your list, estimate how many months or weeks you believe each one will take.

Now, pull out your calendar and begin blocking off the spans of time you are committing to focus on this goal. In Section 2 of your *Time-Blocking Day Planner*, you will find a simple calendar with the months of the year where you can draw out your Macro-Blocks.

The point of this calendar is not to plan down to the very day when you will start and finish this goal because your plans and your estimates for how long these goals will take will most likely be adjusted over time. The purpose is to serve as a general timeline so that you set aside time to work on your essential goals. (Again, you are given multiple pages for this in the *Day Planner* in the likely case you will need to revisit your Macro-Blocks and make revisions.)

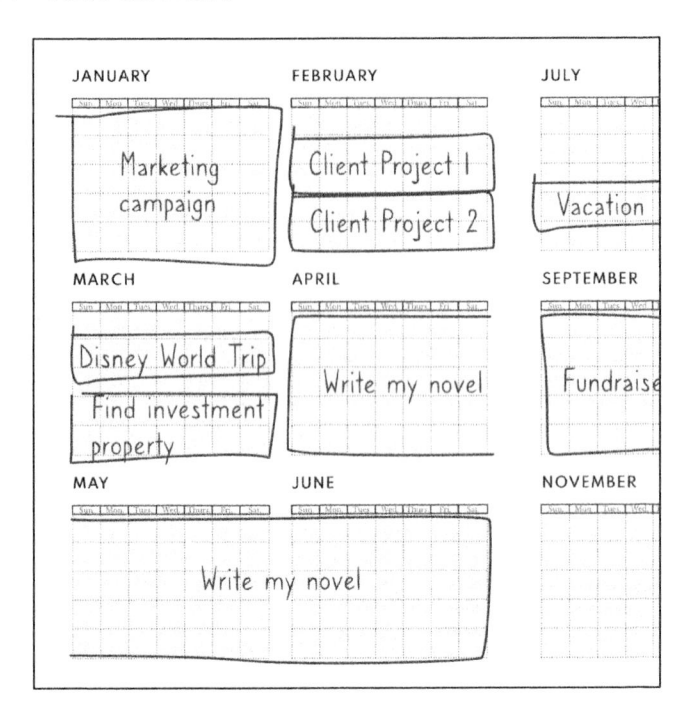

JANUARY Marketing campaign	**FEBRUARY** Client Project 1 Client Project 2	**JULY** Vacation
MARCH Disney World Trip Find investment property	**APRIL** Write my novel	**SEPTEMBER** Fundraise
MAY Write my novel	**JUNE**	**NOVEMBER**

As much as possible, do not overlap your Macro-Blocks. Remember, the purpose is to allow you to focus on a macro level to achieve these goals. You are, in essence saying, "I dedicate the months of January through February to achieving _____."

You may decide to set aside an entire quarter (three months) to a single goal. Some goals may only require a week. Others may require half of the year.

For those goals that will take several months, we can reverse engineer them even further. If you decide that the first half of the year is your time to build an online course, then I recommend creating Macro-blocks that are subsets of the larger block of time. Maybe month one will be set aside to plan content and write scripts, months two through four for filming video content, and months five and six for creating your marketing strategy.

You can continue to break down those Macro-Blocks even smaller if you want to.

This form of Time-Blocking has the big picture in mind to help manage your focus on a larger scale. It will help keep you on track toward achieving your goals over a longer period of time. Our next form of Time-Blocking will help us translate the macro-level goals into micro-tasks to help us accomplish them.

CHAPTER SEVEN

MICRO-BLOCKING

The most common form of Time-Blocking is Micro-Blocking. It is the best method I know for completing any task in the shortest amount of time possible.

Micro-Blocking is the practice of designing blocks of time in your day which you dedicate to a single task or objective. It is saying, for one hour today—or from 1:00–2:30, or for my entire morning—I commit to working on *X task*. The goal of these Time-Blocks is to achieve optimal focus, allowing you to work faster and more efficiently on that task.

As we have discussed, in order to make the most of this time, we must perform one task and one task only. We must maintain single-focus and resist multitasking. We must also set up boundaries around that span of time, cutting off unnecessary communication channels and being ready to say "no" (or at least "not now") to any outside requests that come through.

FROM MACRO TO MICRO

The reason we discussed Macro-Blocking first within the Time-Blocking Method is because it can assist us in discerning what we should Time-Block on the microscopic level. Having set aside several weeks or months to focus on a particular goal, the next step is to use Micro-Blocking to ensure that we take actions every week and every day toward that goal.

What we must do is reverse engineer the goal we have Macro-Blocked for this span of time. Write down the steps it will take to complete this larger goal during the timeframe you designated.

This may be more obvious for certain goals than for others. In writing this book, my steps have been plain and simple: sit down and write every day.

For other goals, like say, launching a new product, reverse engineering the steps may look something like this:

1. Perform market research
2. Develop a Minimum Viable Product (MVP)
3. Do a soft launch to get feedback from early adopters
4. Make a sale to validate the product
5. Prepare a marketing strategy
6. Officially launch the product

Next, decide how much time you will need to commit in order to get it done in the time you've set. How much time do you think you'll *need* to spend? How much time can you realistically afford to spend? Should you Time-Block these tasks every day? Every weekday? Once a week?

Ideally, when working toward a larger goal, I recommend Time-Blocking these tasks every weekday. Doing so will allow you to build them into your schedule and help you develop them as a new habit.

And if this task is one that wouldn't normally fit in the context of your traditional work (for example, if you are an accountant, and your goal is write and record ten songs for an album), Time-Blocking it every weekday can help you to view this task as a real part of your job. You no longer want to view this goal as simply a side-hustle, one you work on haphazardly whenever you get a spare moment. This is a key part of your work, and I believe you deserve to treat it as such.

I also recognize that this may not be realistic for everyone, especially if you have a full-time corporate job or own a business that is very demanding of your time. In these cases, you may have no choice but to Time-Block these tasks just on the weekend. Or perhaps you have a little extra time in the evenings on Monday, Wednesday, and Friday, and you decide to Time-Block an hour on those days.

Of course, the amount of time and the frequency you choose will determine how quickly you are able to reach your goal. That being said, I believe what is more important is that you actually commit to something consistent. You never know—you may be surprised at how much more you are able to accomplish simply by practicing the Time-Blocking Method along with our Five Rules.

LIMIT YOUR TIME

One of the many reasons why the Time-Blocking Method works is actually due to the very fact that it limits you. Often, we think of limits as bad things, but I would challenge this mindset. Some of the most creative solutions and innovations have been developed *because* of the constraints their innovators had to work within.

Like it or not, limits are a part of life, and *time* is one of those limits that none of us can elude. No matter what we seek to accomplish in this life, we only have twenty-four hours per day, seven days per week, 365 days per year. And since we do not have unlimited time, it requires us to set constraints on the way we spend our time.

Perhaps you have heard of the concept of Parkinson's Law, which says that "work expands so as to fill the time available for its completion." In other words, a task will take as long as you give yourself to get it done. If I were your boss, assigning you a task, and gave you a deadline of twenty-four hours to complete it, Parkison's Law dictates that it will take you about twenty-four hours to get it done. However, let's say I give you the same task but instead gave you a deadline of one week to complete it. According to this law, it would actually take you longer to complete.

Why is that? Well, maybe you can recall a time when you were working with a very tight deadline. Maybe it was a school project you had procrastinated, which caused you to scramble to get it done the night before. Or maybe you have had a client or boss give you a seemingly unrealistic deadline to complete a task. What did you have to do to get it done in time? Did you have time to double-check and triple-check your work? Did you have time to make it perfect? Probably not. But you still got it done.

With Parkinson's Law, we find that the more time we have is more time we have to waste. But when given a shorter amount of time to do something, all of a sudden, we are forced to be more resourceful. It often requires us to strip away all the fluff and focus in on doing only what is essential for completing that task. We don't have extra time to overthink, second guess, or make it perfect. Instead, we come away with a result that is perfectly adequate.

Had you been given more time to work on the task, would the result have been better? Maybe . . . but in many cases, no. Such improvements to the final product are usually negligible at best. It is apparent that, left to our own devices with no deadline or limits on our time, we tend to find ways to focus on the non-essentials. We waste time.

The beauty of Time-Blocking is it requires you to set limits on the time you spend on a task. Effective Micro-Blocks have true beginnings and ends.

It is not enough to designate a start time. You must also set an end time. Allowing yourself an indefinite amount of time to work on a task, is only setting yourself up to work twice as long as you need to. Because of Parkinson's Law, you will find that Time-Blocking allows you to achieve more in less time.

THE POWER OF THE TOMATO

With the introduction of his "Pomodoro Technique," Francesco Cirillo shed light on one of the most important Time-Blocking tools at our disposal. *Pomodoro* is actually the Italian word for tomato. Cirillo named his famous method after his tomato-shaped kitchen timer, which he used daily to notify him when his Time-Blocks (or "pomodoros," as he called them) were over. When beginning each task, he would wind up that timer and work until he heard it go off.

Next to your *Time-Blocking Day Planner*, a timer will be the single most important tool you can use. Whether you prefer to use a digital alarm or an old-fashioned kitchen timer is completely up to you. The important thing is that you utilize some sort of device that will let you know it is time to switch tasks.

Simply keeping an eye on the clock will not suffice in Time-Blocking. For one thing, having to constantly look up at the clock to make sure you stay on schedule gives your brain an unnecessary task to focus on. It won't allow you to focus on the task at hand to the full extent.

Another important reason why you should use a timer is that the audible ring or alarm acts as a sort of trigger. It disrupts your focus, and while usually this would be a bad thing, when it is time to switch tasks, it is exactly what your brain needs. It is your brain's cue to stop focusing on what it has been doing for the last thirty to ninety minutes, and either shift focus to something new, or take a break.

So, when that timer goes off, no matter what you're working on—no matter how *close* you tell yourself you are to completing that task—you must stop. I emphasize this because, trust me, this is way easier said than done. When you first start applying this method, you are going to be tempted to silence the alarm and continue working.

One reason this can be such a struggle is because our Micro-Blocks will often be followed by at least a short break. As we discussed in Chapter 4, taking time to rest from our work doesn't come naturally to us, and so it is easy for us to deprioritize it. Our temptation will be to fill these blocks with more work until we retrain ourselves to view these Time-Blocks of rest as crucial to our success.

So, fight the urge to keep working through your scheduled break. When the timer goes off, you must stop!

KNOWING WHEN TO QUIT

Committing to quit when the bell sounds may present a challenge for other reasons. For tasks where you lack the motivation to work, the temptation will be to quit early. These tasks generally include those dreaded ones, which you have been putting off for some time.

This also may include tasks you enjoy doing, where you tell yourself you have to be "in the right frame of mind" to work on them. But this is a lie that we tell ourselves, and it is self-sabotaging. As a creative person, this statement was a crutch I used to lean on, and it simply was an excuse to not treat my craft as a real job. When I wasn't in a state of "flow," I simply wouldn't work on that thing.

Seth Godin confirms there is no such thing as "writer's block" or creative block. He explains this is simply perfectionism in full effect—the feeling that what we are creating is not our best work.[xii] The truth is "the muse" comes and goes and is ultimately unreliable. What you can rely on, however, is the power of simply *showing up*.

When Time-Blocking these tasks, you are making a commitment with yourself to work on them for that span of time—the whole span of time, and not a minute longer—even when you don't feel completely motivated to do it. Time-Blocking can actually serve as the mechanism to get you into that state of flow, even when you are initially *not feelin' it*.

In other cases, you'll find you may have the opposite temptation to work longer than you should. These often involve the tasks that we are most excited about. These may include passion projects that, if we could, we would spend the whole day on. Certainly, if you have the capacity to Time-Block one task for the entire day, by all means, do it! However, for the majority of us who have other responsibilities that can't be ignored for an entire day, it means we must limit the time we spend on our favorite tasks.

If we use the Time-Blocking Method to do this, we can make sure we leave the right amount of time available for other essential tasks. Otherwise, we are likely to lose track of time and work longer than we intended. Time-Blocking helps us set these important limits to manage our focus, as well as our time.

You now know the secret of Micro-Blocking. It is a powerful tool that you can use to carve out time for the tasks you have always wanted to do but somehow have not found time to do. You can Micro-Block learning a foreign language or musical instrument. You can Micro-Block writing a novel or screenplay. You can Micro-Block your workout routine or studying to get your real-estate license or working on your side-hustle.

You can use Micro-Blocking to finally get around to the tasks you've been putting off. You can Micro-Block content creation, such as writing a blog post or filming a video. You can Micro-Block marketing tasks such as scheduling social media posts or cold-calling. You can Micro-Block research, planning, or brainstorming.

Mom entrepreneurs can Micro-Block an hour every day while their little one is napping to work on their business. Busy CEOs can Micro-Block fifteen minutes at the beginning of the workday to pray or meditate. Couples can Time-Block an hour each evening to catch up on each other's day.

And in order to get the most out of these small Time-Blocks, you must make a commitment to employ these tactics to be most productive: You will not allow yourself to multitask. You will close out of all browser tabs. You will shut yourself in a quiet space or close off the world with a pair of headphones. You will cut off all forms of communication, such as emails or texts. You may decide to leave your phone in the car or in the other room. You will maintain single-focus during your Time-Blocks.

You will guard your Time-Blocks ferociously. You will make this appointment with yourself and keep it. As much as it depends on you, you will refuse to reschedule or allow another task to impede on this time you've set aside. You will set a timer and work the full time that you set aside and not a second longer.

Remember, achieving your greatest hopes and dreams is at your fingertips by using this tool to take action. By Micro-Blocking the steps to your goals, you will reach them in no time.

We have one last form of Time-Blocking to discuss, which pulls everything we've learned together so that you are able to be more productive, not just on a single task, but throughout your entire day.

CHAPTER EIGHT

DAY-BLOCKING (PART I)

In our final section of the Time-Blocking Method, we are going to bring together everything that we have learned to optimize our day. Here you will apply all of the principles from Section 1, as well as the Macro and Micro approach to Time-Blocking to design your day-to-day routine and supercharge productivity. Taking this approach will allow you to chip away at your goals daily, while creating more time by focusing on the things that matter most. This is a practice known as Day-Blocking.

As the name suggests, Day-Blocking is Time-Blocking your entire day. It takes an intentional approach to your daily routine by designating multiple Micro-Blocks of tasks throughout the course of the day.

You may choose to apply this to just your workday or to your daily life as a whole. For those who work a conventional job and are given little control over their schedules, Day-Blocking may prove less useful for planning your workday;

however, it can still help you achieve greater focus and productivity in the before-work and after-work hours.

The first time I was introduced to the concept of Time-Blocking, it was through a fellow entrepreneur who owns several gyms in my area. I listened in astonishment as he told me that he would not simply Time-Block business-related tasks but also the mundane daily tasks. He would actually Time-Block playing fetch with his dog in the morning. For someone as busy as he was, he felt that, if he didn't actually block off this activity, it simply wouldn't happen.

To some, scheduling time to play with a pet may sound funny and even a little eccentric, but is it? If something is a priority for you, then why wouldn't you carve out specific time to focus on it?

Time-Blocking even seemingly menial tasks ensures you actually make time for them. Maybe puppy playtime would not be a priority for you, but my guess is there are probably other mundane daily tasks that are important enough to you. Whether it be taking time to listen to an audiobook, going for a jog, enjoying a fruit smoothie, engaging on social media, or reading a story to your child before bed, these tasks—though not necessarily life altering—deserve a slot in your day if they are essential to *you*. Why not Time-Block these tasks in your day?

In addition, Time-Blocking these tasks ensures that we don't spend a disproportionate amount of time on them. Remember, we have an irresistible tendency to waste time without setting limits on ourselves. These initially innocent tasks can quickly turn into distractions and timewasters without setting a definitive end time for them. Through Day-

Blocking, we're able to block off a good but limited amount of time to these tasks, so we don't let them impede on the more mission-critical ones.

As you can see, there are virtually no limits to what you can Time-Block.

In practice, Day-Blocking is fairly simple. It involves a daily planning ritual, using an hour-by-hour calendar, and diagraming literal blocks across the hours or minutes you wish to Time-Block. And as we learned in the previous chapter, it is crucial to set timers or alarms to mark the beginning and end of each block.

Without some guidance, this practice could take upwards of twenty minutes out of your day. Combine this with the additional twenty to forty minutes recommended to plan the entire week, and this could add up to an additional two hours or more per week.

We are not trying to take more time away from your already busy schedule. So, I am going to teach you how you can Time-Block your day in less than sixty seconds per weekday and spend a mere twenty-five minutes total *per week* on planning.

EMBRACE THE ROUTINE

It's time to embrace the routine.

Contrary to popular belief, routines are not just made for the self-proclaimed "creatures of habit." You, too, need to create a daily routine. That's because, no matter who you are, we all are affected by a phenomenon known as *decision fatigue*.

The concept of decision fatigue has been most famously illustrated from a study reported by Jonathan Levav and Shai Danziger on the parole rulings of eight Jewish-Israeli judges in

2010.[xiii] The findings showed that court judges were increasingly more likely to grant inmates' requests for parole in the morning than in the afternoon. In fact, as *New York Times* columnist John Tierney reports, "Prisoners who appeared early in the morning received parole about 70 percent of the time, while those who appeared late in the day were paroled less than 10 percent of the time." And in many cases, inmates with similar sentences and crimes were granted different rulings based on the time of day.

The judges, required to make multiple weighty decisions throughout the course of the day, became victims to decision fatigue. Because of it, their overall judgment waned later in the day, causing them to opt for the simpler, status quo ruling.

In the currency of focus, there are at least three major thieves that rob our proverbial focus bank, two of which we have already discussed: (1) Excessive task-switching, usually caused by interruptions or multitasking, and (2) Prolonged concentration on a task without a break or chance to rest. And the third is decision-making.

Decision fatigue often is not just a product of having to make the big decisions. While big decisions do tend to siphon our metal energy much faster, it is often the many compounded smaller decisions which cause us the most strain by the end of the day.

If I were to ask you what the last decision was you had to make, you may struggle to think of anything from the past twenty-four hours. You may not be thinking about the choice you made between cereal or oatmeal, taking the highway or backroads to work, or wearing your hair up or down today. We are barely cognizant of such insignificant decisions, which we make every single day, but the truth is that they do add up.

In fact, it's estimated that the average person is faced with nearly 35,000 choices on a daily basis.[xiv] That number is shocking, and so it shouldn't come as a surprise how much of a toll that decision-making takes on our mental states.

As seen in this example above, the cost of making too many decisions within a short span of time often results in lapses in our judgment. As you might imagine, this can be detrimental to our ability to be our most productive selves. In our work, when our brain suffers from decision fatigue, it often opts for making choices that are easiest and simplest so as to not exert more energy. However, the easiest choices are not always the best choices.

Decision-making is an inescapable fact of life. But that does not mean we cannot find ways to limit the amount of decisions we must make on a daily basis.

Some of the most successful individuals in the world understand this and do whatever they can to eliminate unnecessary decision-making from the equation. It is the reason why CEOs Steve Jobs and Mark Zuckerberg, as well as the 44th U.S. President, can be seen wearing the exact same outfit every day:

> *You'll see I wear only gray or blue suits. I'm trying to pare down decisions. I don't want to make decisions about what I'm eating or wearing. Because I have too many other decisions to make.*
>
> —President Barack Obama

Aside from dressing like Doug Funny every day, another crucial method to cut down on unnecessary decisions is by Day-Blocking. Day-Blocking provides us with a framework for approaching each day, and it can be customized to each individual. The result of this process is less decision-making because, as we'll find, those daily decisions have already been made in advance. When we approach each day with an already predetermined agenda, we're left with the extra headspace to focus on only the essential decisions.

In this chapter, we will design our ideal day and create a routine that we can repeat like clockwork.

If you find that you are still resistant to the idea of creating a daily routine or schedule, chances are you and I fall into the same group: creatives. To the creative mind, routines seem boring and stifling. We worry that any form of structure may limit our creativity.

I once thought so, too, but it was Steven Pressfield's book, *The War of Art*, that changed my perspective. Pressfield makes a clear distinction between what it means to be a professional and an amateur in the creative space. He quotes W. Somerset Maugham who, when asked whether he wrote on a schedule or not, responded, "I write only when inspiration strikes. Fortunately it strikes every morning at nine sharp." The passage continues,

> . . . *by performing the mundane physical act of sitting down and starting to work, he set in motion a mysterious but infallible sequence of events that would produce inspiration, as surely as if the goddess had synchronized her watch with his. He knew if he built it, she would come.*[xv]

DESIGN YOUR DAY

As we begin creating our routine, you are encouraged to utilize Section 3 of *The Time-Blocking Day Planner* or a similar hour-by-hour planner. As we work to design your ideal day, the *Day Planner* provides multiple pages to work with in case you make mistakes and need to start over from scratch. This will also allow you the opportunity to make adjustments to your schedule at a later time.

I will be covering how to Day-Block your entire day; however, I understand if you chose to only focus on your work hours.

YOUR WORKDAY BLOCK

On the page, I want you to start by blocking off the span of time designated for your work. For those who have a day job, this is most likely already predetermined for you. So, for example, if you work the typical American workday of 9:00 a.m. to 5:00 p.m., then you would draw a box around the time slot of 9:00 a.m. all the way down to the 5:00 slot.

Time		
6 a.m.		
6:30		
7 a.m.		
7:30		
8 a.m.		
8:30		
9 a.m.		
9:30		
10 a.m.		
10:30		
11 a.m.		
11:30		
NOON		
12:30		
1 p.m.		
1:30		
2 p.m.		
2:30		
3 p.m.		
3:30		
4 p.m.		
4:30		
5 p.m.		
5:30		
6 p.m.		
6:30		
7 p.m.		
7:30		
8 p.m.		
8:30		
9 P.m.		
9:30		
10 p.m.		
10:30		
11 p.m.		
11:30–Midnight		

If you're someone who has more control over your work schedule, then now is the time to decide the hours you want to work during an average day. We recognize there can always be exceptions to these hours, but start by choosing a span of time that would reflect your ideal workday.

If, up until this point, you have been very loose with your start and end times from day to day, now is the time to commit to an easily repeatable schedule.

Now that we have determined your workday block, we will begin filling in the space with daily tasks.

YOUR THREE ESSENTIAL BLOCKS

As we learned in Chapter 3, we want to strive for achieving more by doing fewer things each day. And during each workday, we should narrow down to no more than three main things that we will focus on.

Inside the larger block that is your workday, I want you to determine three blocks of time throughout the day that you will eventually fill in with these three tasks. Now, every situation is different, so the way you schedule your three things may be different than mine; however, I want to share my three essential Time-Blocks and explain why this works for me. Copy whatever you like, but more importantly, apply the principles behind it, and craft your schedule to match your situation.

My three essential tasks are Time-Blocked as follows:

- **Task #1** – 9:00 a.m. – 11:30 a.m.
- **Task #2** – 1:00 p.m. – 2:30 p.m.
- **Task #3** – 2:30 p.m. – 4:30 p.m.

Time	
6 a.m.	
6:30	
7 a.m.	
7:30	
8 a.m.	
8:30	
9 a.m.	**Task #1**
9:30	
10 a.m.	
10:30	
11 a.m.	
11:30	
NOON	
12:30	
1 p.m.	**Task #2**
1:30	
2 p.m.	
2:30	
3 p.m.	**Task #3**
3:30	
4 p.m.	
4:30	
5 p.m.	
5:30	
6 p.m.	
6:30	
7 p.m.	
7:30	
8 p.m.	
8:30	
9 P.m.	
9:30	
10 p.m.	
10:30	
11 p.m.	
11:30 - Midnight	

You may notice that I gave the first task of the day the most time. The reason for this is explained by author Gary Keller (a big proponent of Time-Blocking) in his book, *The One Thing*. His revolutionary book can be summed up in answering the defining question, "What's the one thing you can do, such that by doing it, everything else will be easier or unnecessary?"

Keller then proposes that whatever that one thing is—the most important thing you do on that day—should take precedence and be Time-Blocked first.

By this same logic, I have chosen to make Task #1 the slot for the *most essential* of my three essential tasks. I have opted to tackle this first thing in the morning, allowing me to use my optimal energy—or "willpower," as Keller calls it—to work on it. I have also committed more time to this task. You may do well to do the same.

Still, your three essential Time-Blocks will likely look different than mine. One of your regular essential tasks may take only thirty minutes, while another requires four hours of your day. In which case, your three essential Time-Blocks may look something like this:

- Task #1 – 9:00 a.m. – 9:30 a.m.
- Task #2 – 9:30 p.m. – 12:00 p.m. and 1:00 p.m. – 2:30 p.m.
- Task #3 – 2:30 p.m. – 4:30 p.m.

Where you place your three essential Time-Blocks is completely up to you and must fit the type of tasks you have to complete each day. Put some thought into this, but don't worry about making it perfect right now. You can (and most likely will have to) come back and revise it later.

YOUR BLOCKS FOR REST

When I shared my three essential Time-Blocks, did you notice that something was missing?

I (intentionally) forgot to obey one of our core rules of Time-Blocking. I did not "plan to recharge" by scheduling in times of rest. On our Day-Blocking schedule, it's time to add in our breaks.

Obviously, you should break for lunch or any other mealtime, but this will not be enough to achieve maximum productivity. As we discussed previously, the exact frequency of your breaks is something you should test and determine for yourself. But as a starting place, you should generally shoot for taking a break at least every sixty to ninety minutes.

With this in mind, here is what my Day-Blocking schedule *actually* looks like with breaks added:

- Task #1 – 9:00 a.m. – 10:30 a.m.
- **15-Min. Break – 10:30 a.m. – 10:45 a.m.**
- Task #1 (cont'd) – 10:45 a.m. – 11:30 a.m.
- **Lunch Break - 12:00 p.m. – 1:00 p.m.**
- Task #2 – 1:00 p.m. – 2:30 p.m.
- **15-Min. Break – 2:30 p.m. – 2:45 p.m.**
- Task #3 – 2:45 p.m. – 3:45 p.m.
- **15-Min. Break – 3:45 p.m. – 4:00 p.m.**
- Task #3 (cont'd) – 4:00 p.m. – 4:30 p.m.

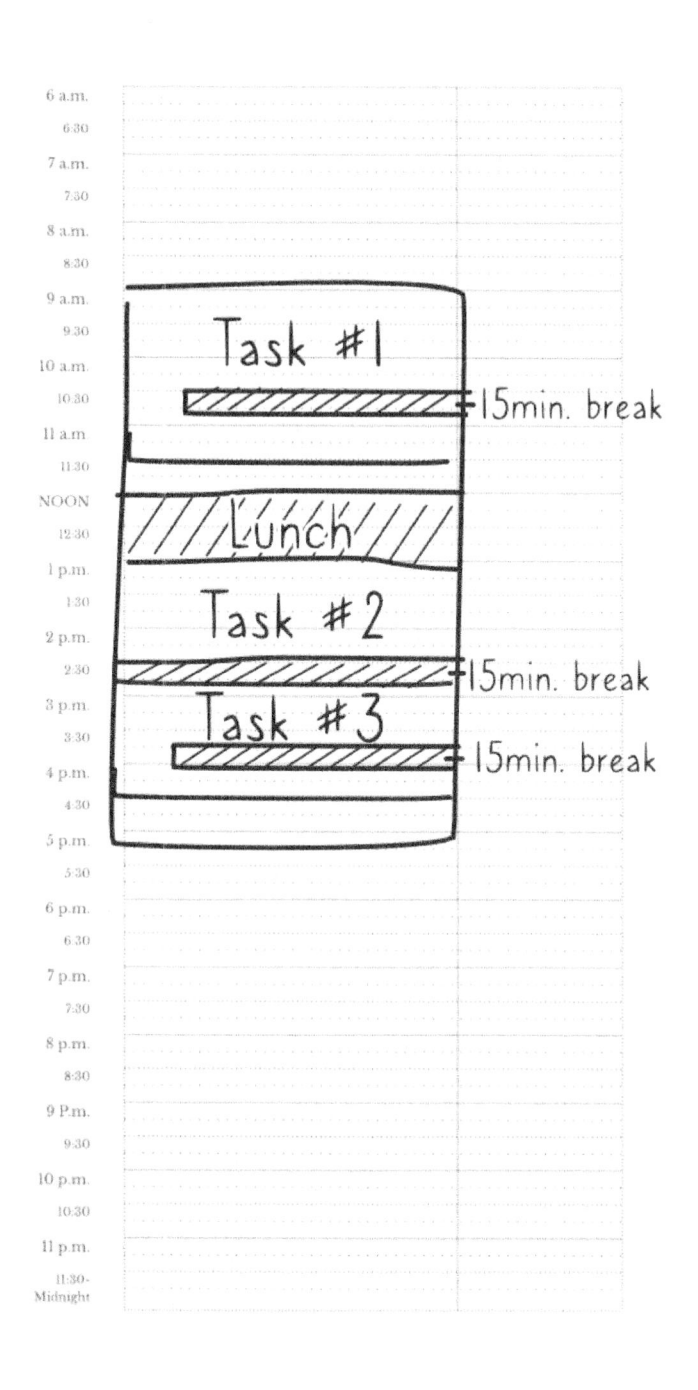

TIME-BLOCKING · 99

Time	
6 a.m.	
6:30	
7 a.m.	
7:30	
8 a.m.	
8:30	
9 a.m.	Task #1
9:30	
10 a.m.	
10:30	15min. break
11 a.m.	
11:30	
NOON	Lunch
12:30	
1 p.m.	Task #2
1:30	
2 p.m.	
2:30	15min. break
3 p.m.	Task #3
3:30	
4 p.m.	15min. break
4:30	
5 p.m.	
5:30	
6 p.m.	
6:30	
7 p.m.	
7:30	
8 p.m.	
8:30	
9 P.m.	
9:30	
10 p.m.	
10:30	
11 p.m.	
11:30 - Midnight	

You will notice that the majority of the breaks are fifteen minutes long, which is an appropriate amount based on the length of time that I work during each sprint. However, if you decide to work in shorter blocks like in the Pomodoro Technique, shorter breaks are fine. The key is to plan breaks in accordance with the amount of time worked. For short Time-Blocks, short breaks should follow. For longer ones, you will need to take longer breaks.

Next, you should also plan a longer break of thirty to sixty minutes for every three to four hours worked. For most of us, this will not be hard since it is already built into the traditional workday. Breaking for lunch can easily serve as this longer break in the middle of the workday. If you have been in the habit of only taking a fifteen-minute lunch break, you should consider extending it. The purpose of this Time-Block is no longer just to eat a meal but to rest your mind and allow you to perform optimally for the second half of the day.

Whenever possible, I generally recommend trying to plan your breaks as a transition between from one task to the next. This allows you to break focus at the right time and shift focus to something new. That being said, it is more important that you actually take breaks between your sixty- to ninety-minute sprints. For example, if you look back at my schedule, Task #1 is usually a task that takes a longer span of time, so I always take a break after the first ninety minutes of working on it then resume that same task for another forty-five minutes.

Time-Blocking your breaks will allow you to form this important habit of resting, giving you a chance to recharge and reset your focus to get the most out of your workday.

So, what should you do during these breaks? The answer is: anything that is not work-related and does not require a lot of focus. Make a cup of coffee or grab a snack. Watch a short YouTube video. Browse social media. If you've been sitting for a while, stand up, stretch, or maybe do some yoga. Meditate. Take a walk or do some push-ups. Play with your dog or cat. Practice an instrument. Draw in a sketch pad. These are just a few ideas.

YOUR COMMUNICATION BLOCKS

The last crucial activity you need to Time-Block in your workday is communication. This block is set aside for checking and responding to email, Slack messages, text messages, voicemail, or any other communication that tends to involve other people imposing their own agendas. If a co-worker attempted to interrupt you earlier in the day, this block of time would be a good time to go see what they needed. If you received an unexpected call while working on a critical task, now is when you can call them back.

Now, I can fill in the final missing slots of my workday with my communication Time-Blocks:

- Task #1 – 9:00 a.m. – 10:30 a.m.
- 15-Min. Break – 10:40 a.m. – 10:45 a.m.
- Task #1 (cont'd) – 10:45 a.m. –11:30 a.m.
- **Email/Other Communication – 11:30 a.m. – 12:00 p.m.**
- Lunch Break - 12:00 p.m. – 1:00 p.m.
- Task #2 – 1:00 p.m. – 2:30 p.m.

- 15-Min. Break – 2:30 p.m. – 2:45 p.m.
- Task #3 – 2:45 p.m. – 3:45 p.m.
- 15-Min. Break – 3:45 p.m. – 4:00 p.m.
- Task #3 (cont'd) – 4:00 p.m. – 4:30 p.m.
- **Email/Other Communication – 4:30 p.m. – 5:00 p.m.**

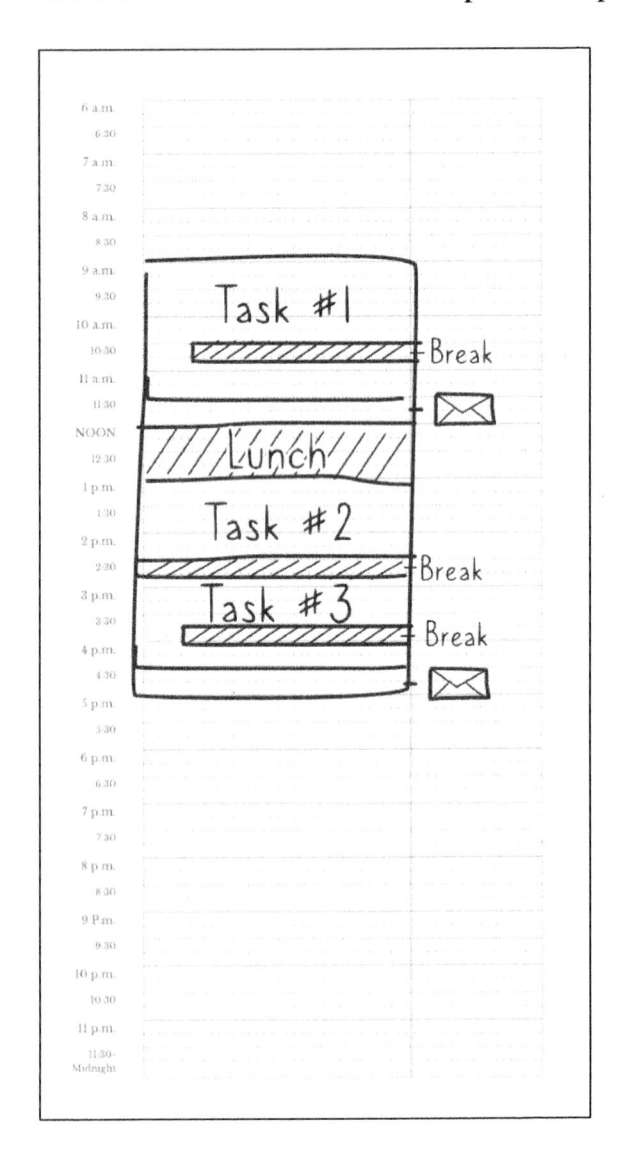

I have set aside only thirty minutes, twice a day—once before lunch and once before quitting time—for checking email and other miscellaneous communication.

It is important to limit this time and make it as short as possible because it is so easy to waste time with tasks like email. Remember, the rule is that you have to stop that task when the timer goes off at the end of the hour. By exploiting Parkinson's Law in this scenario, you are forced to be short and concise with communication, but in the end, it will be more efficient, leaving you more time and energy to focus on the meaningful tasks.

Congratulations, you have officially designed your ideal workday. Next, we are going to design the afterwork hours of your day.

YOUR PERSONAL LIFE BLOCKS

Some may choose to skip this section. The thought of "penciling in" time for playing with your dog, spending time with family, reading a book, or going to the gym may sound like too much. You may feel comfortable sticking to a strict routine for work, but outside of that, you would rather be loose and free to do whatever you feel like. If that is what you choose to do, I completely understand!

But I personally have come to appreciate the philosophy of Time-Blocking as a means to, not only get stuff done but also achieve greater focus on the things that matter. As much as I love what I get to do for work, the things that *really* matter in life often tend to take place outside of the typical workday.

This goes back to understanding your values and the "essentials" that result from those values. If you value spending quality time with your significant other, then why not carve out intentional time for it? If you value being healthy, then why wouldn't you Time-Block going to the gym? Maybe you value a strong spiritual life and you want to block off time for prayer or Scripture reading. If you value your family, you may decide to Time-Block dinners together at the table.

Applying this philosophy to your values, first of all, ensures that you actually carve out the *time* for those things (and make sure they do not get overrun by less important things). If you are like me, and you love what you do for work, it is all too easy to allow work to overrun the things I consider to be essential.

Second, Time-Blocking helps you achieve directed *focus* on the things you value. The mindset of achieving single-focus can be revolutionary in this day and age. Have you ever sat in the living room with the laptop open while your kids were begging for your attention? Have you ever been distracted by a text message alert while out with a friend for coffee? We all have been guilty of these sorts of things because there is no shortage of distractions these days. But is this our best? Don't these people, whom we care about, deserve us to be fully present with them?

No matter what it is you value, I believe you deserve to Time-Block the activities that serve those values.

Here is what my Ideal Day looks like with my personal life blocks:

- Wake Up – 7:30 a.m.
- **Get Ready/Breakfast – 7:30 a.m. 8:30 a.m.**
- **Prayer/Meditation – 8:30 a.m. 9:00 a.m.**
- My Workday – 9:00 a.m. 5:00 p.m.
- **Dinner with Family – 5:00 p.m. 6:00 p.m.**
- **Family Activity – 6:00 p.m. 7:30 p.m.**

- **Put Kids to Bed** – 7:30 p.m. 8:00 p.m.
- **Relax/"Me Time"** – 8:00 p.m. 10:00 p.m.
- **Read a Book Before Bed** – 10:00 p.m. 10:30 p.m.
- Go to Bed – 10:30 p.m.

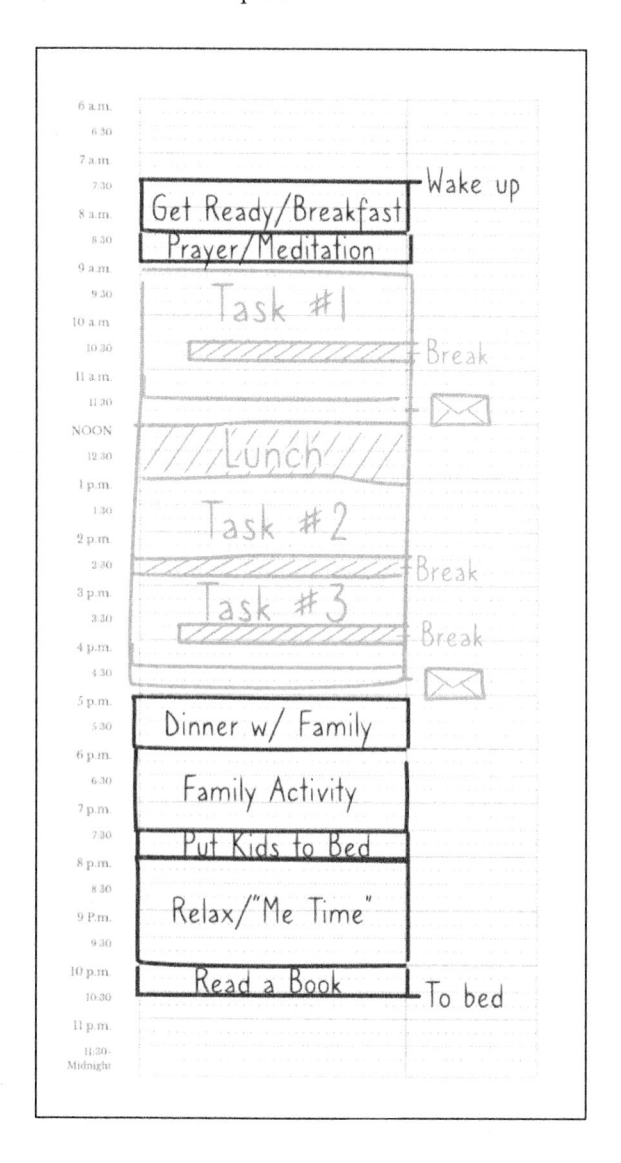

7:30 a.m.	Wake up
8:00 – 8:30 a.m.	Get Ready/Breakfast
8:30 – 9:00 a.m.	Prayer/Meditation
9:00 a.m. – 10:30 a.m.	Task #1
10:30 – 11:00 a.m.	Break
NOON – 1:00 p.m.	Lunch
1:00 – 2:30 p.m.	Task #2
2:30 – 3:00 p.m.	Break
3:00 – 4:00 p.m.	Task #3
4:00 – 4:30 p.m.	Break
5:30 – 6:30 p.m.	Dinner w/ Family
6:30 – 7:30 p.m.	Family Activity
7:30 – 8:00 p.m.	Put Kids to Bed
8:00 – 10:00 p.m.	Relax/"Me Time"
10:00 – 10:30 p.m.	Read a Book
10:30 p.m.	To bed

It is interesting that a true life of freedom actually comes within some boundaries. It seems the default setting is to allow our work, technology, or social media use impede on our essentials. And when we allow these things to keep us from living our purpose and our best life, is that really freedom? But when we use a framework such as Time-Blocking, which in essence puts *limits* on ourselves, we find we are *free* to do the truly important things.

DESIGN YOUR WEEK

Having designed your Ideal Day, you will be able to approach your typical day with a preset plan. However, not every day is going to fit within this initial framework, which is why we can now take a step back and pinpoint any potentially *atypical* days. These are the days that are going to differ drastically from the schedule we created in Section 3 of *The Time-Blocking Day Planner.*

For example, let's say you find that Mondays tend to break up your normal work schedule due to a weekly staff meeting. This meeting would not fit within the Time-Blocks of your Ideal Day, and so Monday would be atypical, or what we'll call a "variant day." You will need to figure out how you can reconcile your routine to make room for these still essential tasks.

Our solution will be to create a weekly routine that allows for these variant days. Like with designing our Ideal Day, the goal is to eliminate unnecessary decision-making and be able to enter each week (and each day of that week) with a set plan. So let's start designing your Ideal Week.

PINPOINT VARIANT WORK TASKS

To start, pinpoint any variant tasks that tend to deter from or break up your schedule. Look back at your Ideal Day schedule, and pinpoint the weekly tasks that would not fit within your Time-Blocks. Let's take a look at your work tasks first.

Examples may include a networking event that occurs from 1:00–3:00 p.m. on Wednesdays. It may be an entire half-day that you set aside to plan your social media content for the week. It may be an entire day that you spend on the golf course with potential clients. Or your business meetings may be your most consistent variant task.

One of my business mentors, Thomas Heath, owns a Personal Branding Firm, and as a part of his business, he regularly schedules coffee meetings with prospects and people he encounters at networking events. These meetings are an essential part of his business, yet they still stand out as variant tasks because they have the potential to break up his day and hinder his productivity.

So, Thomas leverages the Time-Blocking Method to schedule his weekly meetings. He has designed his week, allowing for these meetings to *only* occur on Thursday mornings. In fact, he has designated just three slots to meet whoever wants to pick his brain or connect for business.

Notice a few things about the way he has designed his week. First of all, Thomas only schedules these coffee meetings on one day of the week: Thursday. He graciously offers up his time to others but without forsaking Time-Blocking Rule #5—not letting others dictate this schedule. If someone were to ask to meet any other day of the week, he politely declines, explaining,

"Thursdays are the days that I have set aside for meetings like this."

And while many in his position would simply schedule meetings sporadically throughout the whole day, Thomas knows that this would cost him his focus by causing frequent interruptions in his day and force him to task-switch excessively. Instead, he has designated three forty-five-minute slots back-to-back for coffee meetings. In essence, he batches these three similar tasks into one main Time-Block.

If you have pinpointed any tasks like this that have the potential to interrupt the flow of your Ideal Day, we are going to follow Thomas's example and designate a day out of your week to Time-Block these variant tasks. This will become your variant day.

In Section 4 of your *Time-Blocking Day Planner*, you are provided with separate hour-by-hour calendars for each day of the week. On the day you have designated as your variant day, draw a box extending between the times when you want to tackle this task (or series of tasks) each week.

To give another example from my own schedule: for a time, I would attend the same networking event every Wednesday morning between 9:00 and 10:30. And then, of course, I had to account for the commute, so I made sure to include an extra thirty minutes before and after, making this block of time extend from 8:30–11:00. Wednesday was a "variant day" for me.

It changed my routine, for one, because I had to leave my home office. But more notably, it did not fit within the Time-Blocks I had set for my Ideal Day schedule. If you'll recall, 8:30 a.m. to 9:00 a.m. is my prayer/meditation time, which had to be eliminated on that day. This also meant the earliest I would be able to start on any project would be 11:00 a.m.

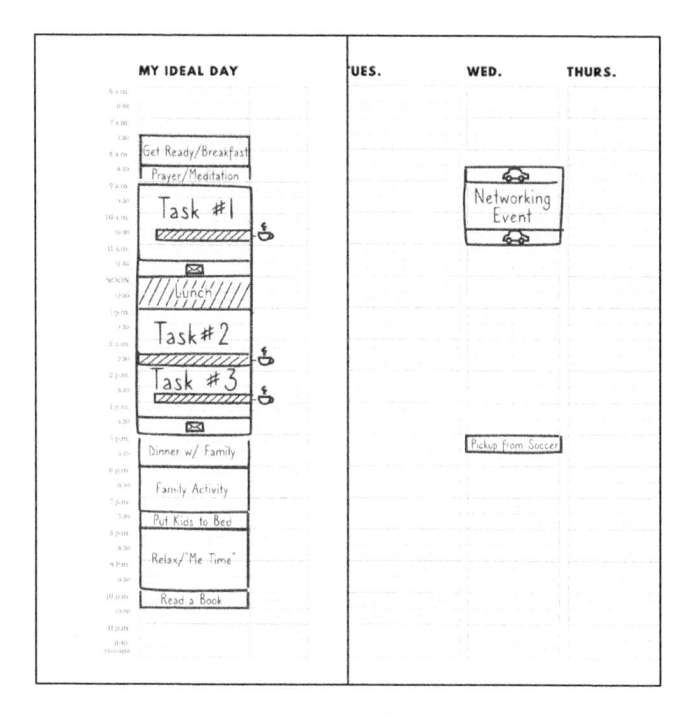

MY IDEAL DAY	TUES.	WED.	THURS.
Get Ready/Breakfast Prayer/Meditation Task #1 Lunch Task #2 Task #3 Dinner w/ Family Family Activity Put Kids to Bed Relax/"Me Time" Read a Book		Networking Event Pickup from Soccer	

It is okay to have more than one variant day of the week—in which case, you will repeat the process on this day in your *Planner*. But I caution you to do so only if absolutely necessary. If you are finding that several days of your week contain activities that conflict with your Ideal Day, you should see if it's possible to move these activities so they all occur on the same day. This way, your brain only has to make that mental shift one day out of the week.

If you cannot do this, you may want to consider revisiting Section 3 and adapt your Time-Blocks accordingly.

I do recognize that, depending on your personality, you may crave more variety in your schedule. Ultimately, do what will work best for you, but just keep in mind that the less consistent your routine is, the more your brain has to work. By designating just one or two days where you divert from your regular routine, you allow your Ideal Days to flow seamlessly. If what you need is a more diverse schedule, opt for changing up the specific tasks and activities you place within each of your essential Time-Blocks, rather than the times themselves.

PINPOINT VARIANT PERSONAL ACTIVITIES

Now, we must simply repeat this process for our personal tasks that occur on a weekly basis.

For example, if you do not go to the gym every day, you will want to Time-Block this activity on whichever days of the week it applies.

Other non-work-related activities may include dropping your child off at soccer practice on only Tuesdays and Thursdays, attending a weekly religious meeting, or engaging in Friday date nights with your spouse. In the same section of our *Time-Blocking Day Planner*, record these activities on the correct day of the week.

FILL IN THE REST OF YOUR WEEK

Now that you have added your variant tasks, you can now fill in the rest of the spaces on your variant days, starting with your work tasks, then moving on to your after-hour activities.

The reason we waited until this point to fill in the rest of our work-related tasks is because, for some, personal activities on these variant days may directly affect your work hours. This will be less common for those working a traditional nine-to-five. However, for the entrepreneurs who have more flexibility with their schedules, this allows you to alter your work hours as needed.

Perhaps, every Tuesday, you need to leave work early to pick up your kids from school at 3:00 p.m., and then resume work from 4:00 p.m. to 6:00 p.m. Or maybe you decide you will quit early every Friday to meet your friends for Happy Hour.

With whatever variant work or personal tasks you have added to your week, now you should adapt the rest of that day around those activities.

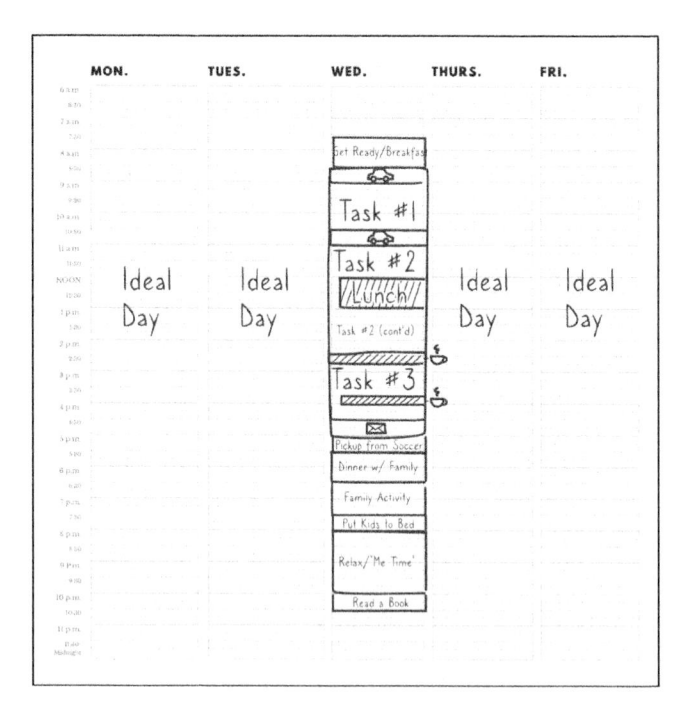

	MON.	TUES.	WED.	THURS.	FRI.
	Ideal Day	Ideal Day	Get Ready/Breakfast Task #1 Task #2 Lunch Task #2 (cont'd) Task #3 Pickup from Soccer Dinner w/ Family Family Activity Put Kids to Bed Relax/"Me Time" Read a Book	Ideal Day	Ideal Day

As you see with the example of my Wednesday networking event, I have adapted the rest of my daily tasks around this new task. First of all, attending this event becomes Essential Task #1 for this particular day. I have kept most of the rest of my routine the same, with the exception of Essential Task #2, which I start upon returning to my desk at 11:00. My commute back from the event serves as my break. And because the event has reduced the amount of time I have to work on other tasks, I have decided to push all of my email communication to the end of the day.

As far as my personal tasks, I included a block for going to pick up my child from soccer practice. Since this interferes with "Dinner with Family" as it is scheduled on my Ideal Day, I adjusted my dinner Time-Block to be from 5:30-6:30 p.m., which also pushes back "Family Time" to start at 6:30.

<u>Wednesday Schedule</u>:

- Wake Up – 7:30 a.m.
- Get Ready/Breakfast – 7:30 a.m. 8:30 a.m.
- **Commute – 8:30 a.m. – 9:00 a.m.**
- **Networking Event (Task #1) – 9:00 a.m. – 10:30 a.m.**
- **Commute/Break – 10:30 a.m. – 11:00 a.m.**
- Task #2 – 11:00 a.m. – 12:00 a.m.
- Lunch Break - 12:00 p.m. – 1:00 p.m.
- Task #2 (cont'd) – 1:00 p.m. – 2:30 p.m.
- 15-Min. Break – 2:30 p.m. – 2:45 p.m.
- Task #3 – 2:45 p.m. – 3:45 p.m.
- 15-Min. Break – 3:45 p.m. – 4:00 p.m.
- Task #3 (cont'd) – 4:00 p.m. – 4:30 p.m.
- Email/Other Communication – 4:30 p.m. – 5:00 p.m.
- **Pick up Kid from Soccer – 5:00 p.m. – 5:30 p.m.**
- Dinner with Family – 5:30 p.m. 6:00 p.m.
- Family Activity – 6:00 p.m. 7:30 p.m.
- Put Kids to Bed – 7:30 p.m. 8:00 p.m.
- Relax/"Me Time" – 8:00 p.m. 10:00 p.m.

- Read a Book Before Bed – 10:00 p.m. 10:30 p.m.
- Go to Bed – 10:30 p.m.

Now in your *Day Planner*, you can fill in your Ideal Days, which should be blank at this point. You may either fill in all the blocks you wrote out previously for your Ideal Day, which will allow you to see your entire Ideal Week at a glance; or you can simply write "Ideal Day" on the column for that particular day, and you will know to refer back to your Ideal Day page you filled out in Section 3.

Now, having designed both your Ideal Day and Ideal Week, you will be able to approach each day with an existing outline for how to make the most out of it.

Your Ideal Day/Week can and should be revisited as your daily life changes and as your goals shift. This is why we have provided multiple pages in the *Day Planner*, allowing you to design and redesign your routine as needed throughout the year.

With that said, let's take our new routine, and begin applying it now.

CHAPTER NINE

DAY-BLOCKING (PART II)

Now it's time to get into the nitty gritty of Day-Blocking. To make sure we are staying focused on our essentials and Time-Blocking the right things, I strongly recommend spending around ten to twenty minutes planning your week. This can be done first thing Monday morning, on Sunday evening before you start your week, or even on Friday as your final task before beginning the weekend.

To make this process quick and easy, in *The Time-Blocking Day Planner* we have provided two pages at the beginning of each week to guide you.

PLAN YOUR WEEK

WEEKLY GOALS

Step one is to write out all of your goals for this week only. These should encompass your most important high-level tasks. Ask yourself, what absolutely needs to get done? If you were to come to the end of this week without having achieved certain outcomes, which of those would cause you the most regret? Write those things down here.

During this time, you should also take a second to look back at your goals that you wrote down for this year (Section 1 in your *Day Planner*).

For starters, if you have already chosen to Macro-Block a larger goal, make sure you know what that goal is. Then, to ensure that you are taking steps toward meeting at least one of your large goals, write down a smaller sub-goal here that you can work on this week. You should have already reverse engineered several of the steps to meet your larger goal, so use this as a guide to determine what smaller goal you should tackle this week.

In your *Day Planner*, you are provided with space for up to six goals. This is not any sort of magic number; it is only a limit. In many cases, choosing six high-level tasks to complete will actually be unrealistic. The number will change from week to week, and in some weeks, you may find that just focusing on one single goal is plenty.

Keeping in mind that you only have seven days to accomplish these goals (or five business days), do they fit into your SMART Goals framework?

Try to be very specific with these goals, especially if it is part of a larger project that you would not be able to complete within the week. For example, rather than saying "Redesign my website," use a more measurable goal like, "Complete three pages of my new website." Instead of saying "Work on my book," say, "Write 8,000 words of my book."

"SAID IT" AND FORGET IT LIST

As you are brainstorming these goals, you will most likely be reminded of those *other* tasks that tend to linger in the mind: drop off a package at the post office, reply to that email, return a phone call, order a birthday present, and so on. It is only natural that these minor tasks pop into your brain. It is, in fact, your brain trying not to forget them.

But what we cannot do is allow these less essential tasks to overrun our thoughts. And what we *absolutely* cannot let them do is become the "squeaky wheel that gets the grease." Just because they are taking up our headspace at the moment does not mean they deserve precedent over our high-level tasks for the week.

The solution, as we discussed in Chapter 3, is to add these items to your *Said It and Forget It List*. You'll find a page right beside your Weekly Goals list in *The Time-Blocking Day Planner* that serves this purpose. Remember, this is your To-Do list of non-essential tasks. Adding tasks to this list allows your brain to chill out because it knows it no longer has to do the work of remembering the tasks because the pen and paper are doing that for you.

The key to this stage of planning is thinking critically about which tasks truly belong on your list of goals for this week and which ones you can just "get to it if you have the time" or put off for another week. This is not easy, and frankly, it requires us to be brutally honest with ourselves.

If I don't get this task done, will the world really end?

Sure, there *will* be consequences—every action (and inaction) has a consequence. But the question is, can you live with the consequences of not getting to that task this week?

In contrast, can you live with the consequences of *not* having taken steps toward your essential goals? This is why it's so important to take this ten to twenty minutes to clarify which is which.

Another way you may choose to approach this is to write out your entire list of to-dos on the page first. This can often help you better judge the essentials from the non-essentials to see all of the tasks written out. Then simply circle the items you deem to be the essential goals for that particular week and add those to your Week's Goals.

Keep in mind that your *Said It and Forget It List* is a tool that can be used throughout the week. Any time a new To-Do pops into your head, you can quickly jot it down then get back to what you were doing. However, this list is intentionally placed on a separate page that is not visible to you during the week when you're filling out your Day-Blocking sheet. This list needs to remain out of sight so that these tasks do not become a distraction or a worry.

If you happen to crush all of your goals for that week, then by all means, come back to this list and start checking them off, too. If you get to them, great! But if not, remember, it's not the end of the world.

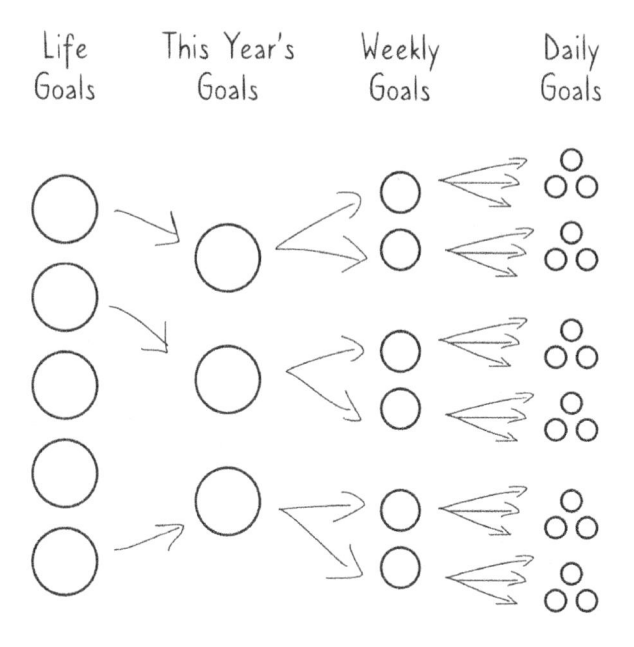

Life Goals	This Year's Goals	Weekly Goals	Daily Goals

REVERSE ENGINEERING ONE LAST TIME

We started the Time-Blocking Method by reverse engineering your Life Goals into goals for this year. We reverse engineered your Year's Goals into weekly goals. Now, it is time to reverse engineer your goals one more time, so you can know the sub-tasks you need to Micro-Block within your day.

In your *Planner*, underneath your Week's Goals, I want you to write out the individual steps that will allow you to accomplish that goal within the week. While some of these goals may be straight-forward enough to complete in one sitting and not involve a bunch of steps, the majority of them will involve multiple steps due to their high-level nature.

> ☐ **GOAL #1**
> New website - 3 pages
>
> **Steps** *(Reverse Engineered)*:
> o Write website copy
> o Design icons
> o
>
> ☐ **GOAL #2**
> Write 8000 words for manuscript
>
> **Steps** *(Reverse Engineered)*:
> o Day 1: Write for 2 hrs.
> o Day 2: Write for 2 hrs.
> o Day 3: Write for 2 hrs.
>
> ☐ **GOAL #3**
> Create video content
>
> **Steps** *(Reverse Engineered)*:
> o Film
> o Send to editor
> o Post on social media
>
> ☐ **GOAL #4**
>
> **Steps** *(Reverse Engineered)*:
> o
> o
> o

From this point, we have a roadmap for our entire week. Now, it's time to Time-Block our day.

TIME-BLOCKING YOUR DAY

On the next five pages of your *Day Planner*, you will find an hour-by-hour calendar for each day of the workweek. Each morning, before you start on any task, you will go through the simple process of "Day-Blocking" by filling out this sheet. Because we have already laid the groundwork for what your Ideal Week will look like, filling it out should be a breeze and take no more than sixty seconds each day.

Start by writing the date at the top.

Next, on the left side of the page, you will find three slots with a checkbox where you will jot down your three essential tasks for the day.

Here is where you will fill in the sub-tasks/steps that you wrote down on your Weekly Planning page.

```
┌─────────────────────────────────────────┐
│                          6 a.m.         │
│      MONDAY              6:30           │
│                          7 a.m.         │
│   Today's Date:          7:30           │
│                          8 a.m.         │
│   01 / 03 / 2022         8:30           │
│                          9 a.m.         │
│   ☐ TASK #1              9:30           │
│                          10 a.m.        │
│   Review Client          10:30          │
│   Blog Posts             11 a.m.        │
│                          11:30          │
│   ☐ TASK #2              NOON           │
│                          12:30          │
│   Write website          1 p.m.         │
│   copy                   1:30           │
│                          2 p.m.         │
└─────────────────────────────────────────┘
```

One thing you may be wondering is how you should handle tasks that don't take that much time. For these instances, you want to take advantage of something called "batching." Since *focus* is always the driving force behind our Time-Blocks, we want to couple as many tasks as possible in one slot, ones that all have a similar focus.

For example, within my agency, we create blog content for several of our clients. So, one of my recurring tasks is reviewing the blog posts that I've assigned one of my contractors to write.

In a given week, I may have to review two blog posts for one client and two posts for another client. Now, technically, I could view this as being four separate tasks (since they technically are); but the problem is that it generally takes me less than thirty minutes per post, so it would not make sense to dedicate an entire ninety-minute Time-Block to reviewing a single post.

So, what do I do? I wait until multiple blog post drafts have been completed and then set aside one Time-Block on one day of the week for reviewing all of the blog posts in a single "batch." So, if I were to make this one of my three tasks for the day, I would probably write something like "Review Client Blog Posts" in the task slot.

Another great use of batching could be creating social media content. If you create content for your social media accounts, the way most of us go about this is by carving out a small amount of time each day to create one piece of content and manually posting it. But a more effective method would be to Time-Block your social posts for the week. Within that block, you would create a week's worth of posts, so they are ready to go. And in most cases, you can even utilize online software to schedule these posts. Think of how much time and energy you save by batching these tasks for an hour or so on one day per week, rather than have to worry about it on each individual day.

In *The Time-Blocking Day Planner*, you are also provided with space under your three tasks to make note of any appointments you need to take into account for that day.

FILL IN YOUR BLOCKS

Based on your "Ideal Week" schedule that you designed, the next step is to draw out your blocks in the correct time slots for that day of the week. Refer back to Section 4 of the Day Planner and draw your blocks accordingly. Draw your Three Essential Blocks, your Blocks for Rest, your Communication Blocks, and any activities that occur before and after work.

Next, decide which of your three main tasks for the day belong in which of your three essential blocks. You can write them on the block if you want, but I recommend simply marking it with a #1, #2, and #3 to save time.

Now, how do you decide which task should go in which block?

What I will tell you is the order in which you tackle each of these three tasks does actually matter; however, there is no one answer to this question.

As previously mentioned, Gary Keller's *The One Thing* challenges readers to determine that *one* task or activity that, by focusing on it, will make all other tasks easier or unnecessary. To use his own metaphor, your "one thing" is the big domino that, once knocked down, will cause all of the other dominos to fall into place. In the context of Time-Blocking, this task would be the *most* essential of your three essential tasks that day. Keller recommends that *this* be the very first task you work on every single day.

MONDAY

Today's Date: 01 / 03 / 2022

☐ **TASK #1**
Review Client Blog Posts

☐ **TASK #2**
Write website copy

☐ **TASK #3**
Film video

Appointments:

🕐 __:__ - __:__
_____

🕐 __:__ - __:__
_____

🕐 __:__ - __:__
_____

🕐 __:__ - __:__
_____

6 a.m.	
6:30	
7 a.m.	
7:30	
8 a.m.	Get Ready/Breakfast
8:30	Prayer/Meditation
9 a.m.	
9:30	#1
10 a.m.	
10:30	///////// ☕
11 a.m.	
11:30	✉
NOON	
12:30	//// Lunch ////
1 p.m.	
1:30	
2 p.m.	#2
2:30	///////// ☕
3 p.m.	#3
3:30	///////// ☕
4 p.m.	
4:30	✉
5 p.m.	
5:30	Dinner w/ Family
6 p.m.	
6:30	Family Activity
7 p.m.	
7:30	Put Kids to Bed
8 p.m.	
8:30	Relax/"Me Time"
9 P.m.	
9:30	
10 p.m.	Read a Book
10:30	
11 p.m.	
11:30-Midnight	

Author Brian Tracy shares a similar philosophy, but with a slightly different twist. Tracy has coined the phrase, "Eat that frog!"[xvi] which is a challenge to pinpoint the *hardest* thing you have to do for the day (the "frog") and complete that first. This often tends to be the thing we have been putting off, which makes it a great remedy for procrastination. Tracy suggests that completing this task first makes the rest of your day all the easier.

These two philosophies differ slightly in that your "one thing" and your "frog" could be two different things; however, in many cases, they are one in the same. Where I wholeheartedly agree with Keller's "One Thing" philosophy, my only caution with "eating the frog" is that you take a second to contemplate whether your proverbial frog is actually one of your essentials. Just because a task is hard does not necessarily make it essential. And if it's not essential, then it's not worth Time-Blocking as one of your Three Tasks. At the same time, it could be that the task you have been procrastinating is one that is vital to your success.

What both of these approaches have in common is an attempt to leverage the peak of your focus energy by doing the task first. It recognizes that your energy is going to deplete over the course of the day. However, Daniel Pink, author of the book *When*,[xvii] tells us that there are different kinds of focus energy and that our drive to work on different kinds of tasks actually ebbs and flows throughout the day.

For example, you may find you have more creative energy during the morning hours of the day. This is energy that could be used for writing a book or designing something. During the afternoon, you have more analytical and problem-solving energy for tasks such as research or bookkeeping. According to

Pink, these different types of energies will be higher at different times of the day, depending on the individual.

As you begin Day-Blocking, be mindful of your energy and motivation levels so you can discover when may be the best times for you to work on certain tasks.

So, to get back to answering the question of what order you should arrange your Three Essential Tasks, I believe you can use a combination of these three philosophies to discern what will work best for your unique personality.

If you *can* tackle your most important task of the day first, this would be my recommendation. Doing this will ensure that (1) it actually gets done, without the possibility of other tasks getting in the way, and (2) you will be able to commit the firstfruits of your energy to it. However, if you come to discover that your peak hours to work on a certain task actually occurs later in the day, then Time-Block this task at that optimal time!

Next, let's take a look at your breaks.

In your Time-Blocks designated for breaks, I recommend writing down exactly what you plan to do during that time. For me, I'm a drummer, and I keep a drum pad in my office, so during my first fifteen-minute break, I often spend time practicing drum rudiments. I will write that down as "Practice Drums" in that slot. In addition, I always set aside an hour for my lunch break, but during the latter thirty minutes, I often like to take a walk; and during my first fifteen-minute break in the afternoon, I always enjoy a second cup of coffee. So, I write each of these in the appropriate slot.

Since taking these additional breaks may be new for you, I encourage you to plan an activity you can look forward to. Just make sure it is one that will still allow your mind to rest and reset.

Once you're finished filling out each of your Time-Blocks, it's time to rock and roll!

Don't forget to utilize your timer. The whole system falls apart without this tool because you need some sort of trigger to let you know it's time to stop what you're doing and move on to the next block.

To make it even easier, you may want to set alarms on your device to notify you when it is time to task-switch. Since you have already designed each day of your week, you can predictably set up these alarms for the exact day and time that corresponds with the start of each Time-Block. I've often taken this approach, and I find that it saves me the most time and energy because I don't have to think about it. However, others may find that a more traditional timer is more suitable for them.

YOUR FIRST 2 WEEKS

Since this will be your first experience with Day-Blocking, there's something I want you to do just for the first two weeks. I want you to take a little extra time to record the Time-Blocks for what you planned to do, as well as the blocks for what actually happened.

In *The Time-Blocking Day Planner*, you will notice that each Day-Blocking page provides two columns. This is so you have space to record your initial plan in the first column, and then you can use the second column to draw out the blocks of what you actually did that day.

128 · LUKE SEAVERS

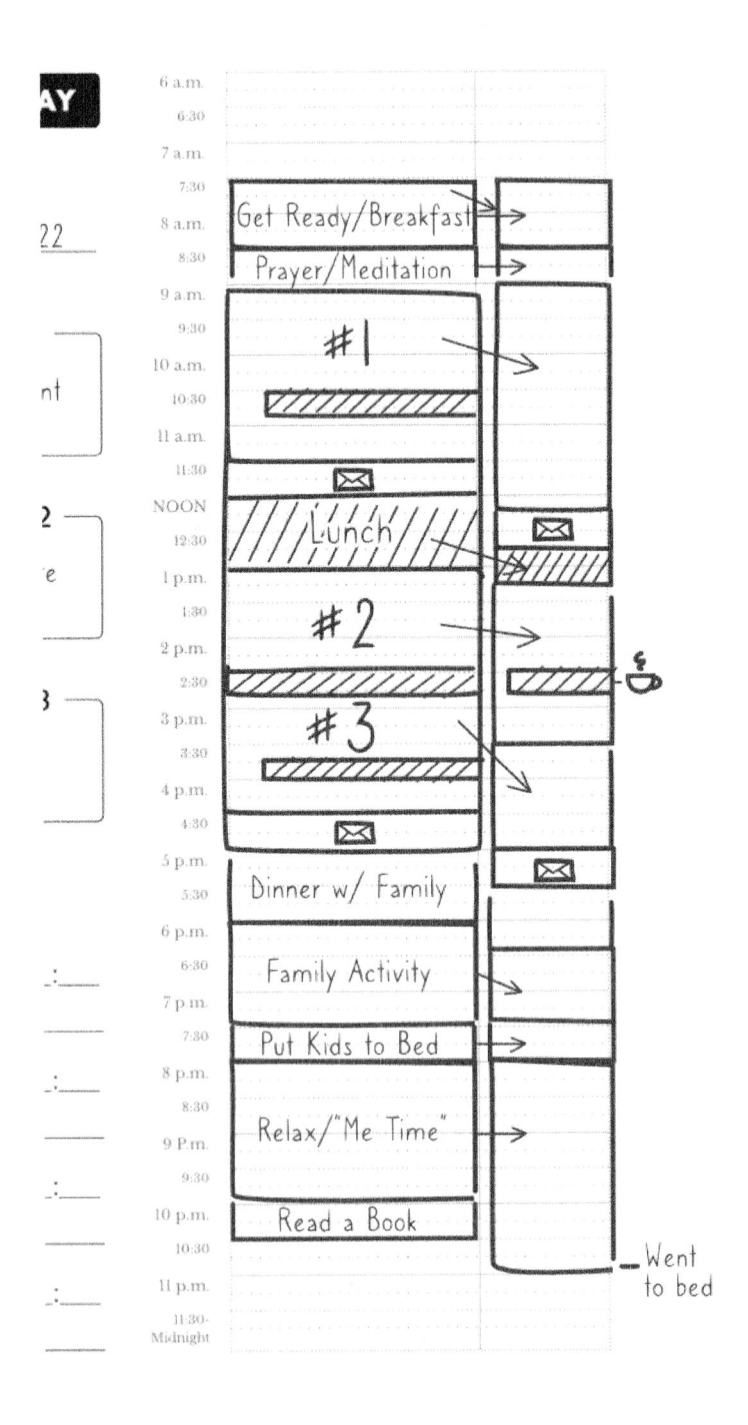

6 a.m.		
6:30		
7 a.m.		
7:30		
8 a.m.	Get Ready/Breakfast →	
8:30	Prayer/Meditation →	
9 a.m.		
9:30	#1	
10 a.m.		
10:30	▨▨▨▨	
11 a.m.		
11:30	✉	
NOON	//// Lunch ////	✉
12:30		▨▨
1 p.m.		
1:30	#2	
2 p.m.		
2:30	▨▨▨▨	▨▨ ☕
3 p.m.	#3	
3:30	▨▨▨▨	
4 p.m.		
4:30	✉	
5 p.m.		✉
5:30	Dinner w/ Family	
6 p.m.		
6:30	Family Activity	
7 p.m.		
7:30	Put Kids to Bed →	
8 p.m.		
8:30	Relax/"Me Time" →	
9 P.m.		
9:30		
10 p.m.	Read a Book	
10:30		
11 p.m.		— Went to bed
11:30-Midnight		

This will contribute to your future success in two ways:

One, it will allow you to see what areas you need to improve on. The entire mindset and method of Time-Blocking can take some getting used to, as it often tends to buck against the schedule that we've become accustomed to. Whether you find yourself not taking breaks, checking email in the middle of tasks, or breaking any of the other Time-Blocking rules, it's important to record those activities during these two weeks. It will bring to light the key areas you need to gradually improve upon if you want to be your most productive self.

Two, this two-week trial period will allow you to put your Ideal Day and Ideal Week to the test. After the two weeks, you will be able to look and see whether or not this routine you designed for yourself is working for you. At that point, you will be able to revisit your Time-Blocking schedule and make any necessary adjustments.

In the likely case that you have never done an hour-by-hour analysis of your daily activities, what you'll most likely find is the Planning Fallacy in full effect. There are certain tasks you may find in which you overestimated the time they took. But more often than not, you will see how prone you are to *underestimate* how long certain tasks will take you.

By choosing only three primary tasks to focus on each day, we can hope to avoid many of the pitfalls of the Planning Fallacy. However, you can use these first two weeks to pay close attention to how long your specific tasks take you. This will allow you to better plan your Time-Blocks to match your individual workflow.

If you find you are finishing tasks quicker than you anticipated, you may be able to batch more similar tasks within your Time-Blocks.

If you are not completing everything you meant to, it may require that you do a better job dividing tasks up into subtasks and assigning less to yourself. Remember, we want to set ourselves up for success, not for failure. We want to shoot to achieve small wins that will motivate us to eventually achieve bigger wins.

Once you have completed these two weeks, I encourage you to revisit your Ideal Day and Ideal Week and see if you need to redesign your Time-Blocks based on what you learned.

THE FLEXIBILITY OF TIME-BLOCKING

With this, you have all of the tools you need to be successful in Time-Blocking to supercharge productivity.

But Time-Blocking daily and following the rules of Time-Blocking is no easy task. Multitasking, working through breaks, and trying to accomplish *everything*, frankly, are difficult habits to break. Not to mention, you will be met with many outside influences that are products of a culture that does not value these principles.

In many ways, the odds are against you on your productivity journey, and it's very likely that you will mess up. You will not start out Time-Blocking perfectly and will likely still encounter common pitfalls, even years after practicing it. But this should not discourage you.

For me, Time-Blocking has been a game-changer but even I am not perfect at it. There are still days where I jump into work without planning my Time-Blocks. There are still days where I choose to ignore the timer when it goes off and keep working on a task.

I am here to tell you that you will make mistakes, but it's OK. Failing should not be an indication that these principles don't work or that you should give up trying. If anything, it's simply a reminder that you are human.

Start each new day fresh, try to implement these tools, and you will get better over time. Even if you only implemented half of the principles found in this book, you will still see major improvements in your productivity!

And the reality is, even if we all followed this method to a *T*, there will always be circumstances outside of our control that will sometimes interfere with our plans: we have to quit early for a family emergency. A client comes to us with a truly earth-shattering need. We get caught in traffic. A piece of hardware stops working, and we have to spend the entire day getting it fixed.

But the beauty of Time-Blocking is that it is extremely flexible. The second column on your Day-Blocking pages is there for just these circumstances. If (and when) you have to alter your plan, this column is where you can make those adjustments to keep moving forward with your day.

If you do end up completing your Three Essential Tasks earlier than expected, great! Again, you can use the second column to adjust your Time-Blocks accordingly. At this point, you can look back at your *Said It and Forget It List* and begin tackling some of these, if you wish. However, considering that you have determined these items to be non-essential, maybe you don't. Maybe you decide to quit early, spend more time with family, and enjoy life. The choice is up to you!

In the end, the Time-Blocking Method is merely a set of guidelines, and it is here for your benefit. Simply, do your best, and don't sweat the rest.

Productivity is a journey, not a destination. Becoming more productive should never become an end in itself, and so you should give yourself the grace and flexibility to learn and grow along the way. Rather, productivity should be seen merely as a vehicle for reaching your ultimate goals and aspirations. It is my hope that as you begin Time-Blocking your day, you will be empowered to accomplish just that.

FINAL THOUGHTS

It has been my joy to share this incredible tool with you.

I firmly believe that as you begin to plan out and execute on your day through Day-Blocking, you will be able to achieve incredible results. But even if you choose to simply Micro-Block certain tasks or Macro-Block your larger goals, the principles you've learned in this book are ones you will be able to apply to your work and your life, regardless.

For me, I love Time-Blocking as a method; however, I think it has ultimately been the mindset of Time-Blocking that has been most impactful for me.

The simple act of *maintaining a single-focus* and stopping the multitasking has been revolutionary in this world that is always fighting for our focus.

Knowing my life's essentials and being able to commit my focus to *those* things is what has allowed me to live out my life with meaning and purpose.

The counterintuitive truth that I can actually *achieve more by doing less* has been freeing.

The simple practice of *resting* is going to pay dividends in the long run, not only by helping me to stay productive, but also to avoid burnout.

And being able to finally *take back control of my time* to apply these principles has been incredibly empowering.

Following this mindset has been life-changing, giving me *more* time and *better quality* time with my family. It has improved my work performance and allowed me to do more things with my time that align with my passions. It has allowed me to write this book in only a few months while still balancing client work, growing a startup, and maintaining a good family life.

Time-Blocking is a tool that can help you achieve similar outcomes.

I am excited to continue growing, using this incredible system to accomplish more of my goals, and improve my quality of life. I am likely even *more* excited to hear how you are able to do the same!

If you haven't yet, you can pick up your copy of *The Time-Blocking Day Planner*, which is available at timeblockingbook.com.

Since tools and technology are constantly evolving and changing, I have intentionally refrained from referencing many outside resources in this book in an effort to keep the content of this book evergreen; but I have compiled a list of additional resources that you may find helpful on your productivity journey and as you go about Time-Blocking. These tools are also available at timeblockingbook.com.

Lastly, I would love to hear from you! If this book has helped you in any way, please reach out to me at timeblockingbook.com, and share your story.

With that, if you would be so kind as to leave a review of this book on Amazon.com, this will be a huge help to me and allow me to continue spreading the word about Time-Blocking.

The fact is that *there just isn't enough time in the day*, which makes time a truly precious resource. But you now have the tool you need to supercharge productivity, manage your focus, and make the most with this limited resource.

Now, go and reach your goals!

ABOUT THE AUTHOR

LUKE SEAVERS resides in Charleston, SC with his wife and three daughters. Luke is a creative at heart, with a love for writing, music, film, and design. But it is his purpose of serving and empowering the poor that drives him in all of his endeavors.

He and his wife spent time living abroad in Haiti, and eventually founded the non-profit, Home For The Nations. Today, they continue to work amongst impoverished communities there.

These combined passions led Luke into the world of entrepreneurship, starting and building multiple businesses over time. These ventures have not only allowed him to put his creative marketing skills to good use, but also provided a means to give back and continue to advocate for the *least of these*.

But, in wearing so many hats, the need for managing his time—and more importantly, his *focus*—led him to discover the productivity method known as "Time-Blocking." In sharing this powerful tool, it is Luke's hope that this book is able to empower other *world changers* to achieve greater focus in their work and life, and ultimately, accomplish their greatest goals and dreams.

Also available on Amazon:

TIME BLOCKING

DAY PLANNER

A companion to
the book *Time-Blocking*
by Luke Seavers

END NOTES

[i] *Bill Gates and Elon Musk share a daily scheduling habit that helps them tackle their busy routines*, https://www.businessinsider.com/bill-gates-elon-musk-scheduling-habit-2017-8

[ii] Staughton, John. "Can Humans Actually Multitask?" Science ABC, 20 Oct 2019, accessed 17 Dec 2020, https://www.scienceabc.com/humans/can-humans-actually-multitask.html.

[iii] Hyman, Jr., Ira E., et. al. "Did You See the Unicycling Clown? Inattentional Blindness while Walking and Talking on a Cell Phone," Western Washington University in *Applied Cognitive Psychology*, 19 Oct 2009, access 17 Dec 2020, https://msu.edu/course/psy/802/altmann/802/Ch3-4b-HymanEtAl10.pdf.

[iv] McKeown, Greg. *Essentialism*. New York: Currency Publishing, 2019

[v] Mccullough, Brian. "The Incredible True Story Behind AMC's Halt And Catch Fire – How Compaq Cloned IBM And Created An Empire," Internet History Podcast, episode aired 26 May 2014, accessed 17 Dec 2020, http://www.internethistorypodcast.com/2014/05/the-incredible-true-story-behind-amcs-halt-and-catch-fire-how-compaq-cloned-ibm-and-created-an-empire/.

[vi] Ferriss, Timothy. "The Art of Letting Bad Things Happen (and Weapons of Mass Distraction)," *The Tim Ferriss Show*, 25 Oct 2017, accessed 17 Dec 2020, https://tim.blog/2007/10/25/weapons-of-mass-distractions-and-the-art-of-letting-bad-things-happen/

[vii] Matthew 6:34 (New International Version), see copyright page for permissions.

[viii] Beuhler, Roger, et. al. "Exploring the "Planning Fallacy": Why People Underestimate Their Task Completion Times," *Journal of Personality and Social Psychology*, 10 Feb 1994, accessed 17 Dec 2020, http://web.mit.edu/curhan/www/docs/Articles/biases/67_J_Personality_and_Social_Psychology_366_1994.pdf.

[ix] Wade, Francis. "Techniques for Time Blocking Your Calendar," The School for Task Scheduling Blog, accessed 17 Dec 2020, https://scheduleu.org/the-history-of-total-task-scheduling/.

[x] Gifford, Julia. "The secret of the 10% most productive people? Breaking!" DeskTime, 14 May 2018, accessed 17 Dec 2020, https://desktime.com/blog/17-52-ratio-most-productive-people.

[xi] Ferriss, Timothy. *The 4-Hour Work Week: Escape 9–5, Live Anywhere, and Join the New Rich,* New York: Harmony, 2009.

[xii] "Creative Block is a Myth – Seth Godin in One Minute," posted 6 Jan 2019, https://www.youtube.com/watch?v=VRdFjL_uNoo.

[xiii] Danziger, Shai, et al. "Extraneous Factors in Judicial Decisions," *PNAS,* 25 Feb 2011, accessed 17 Dec 2020, https://www.pnas.org/content/pnas/108/17/6889.full.pdf.

[xiv] Sahakian, B. J. and Labuzetta, J. N. *Bad Moves: How Decision Making Goes Wrong, and the Ethics of Smart Drugs.* London: Oxford University Press, 2013.

[xv] Pressfield, Steven. *The War of Art: Break Through the Blocks and Win Your Inner Creative Battle,* Warner Books, 2003.

[xvi] Tracy, Brian., *Eat That Frog!: 21 Great Ways to Stop Procrastinating and Get More Done in Less Time,* Oakland: Berrett-Koehler Publishers, 2017.

[xvii] Pink, Daniel H. *When: The Scientific Secrets of Perfect Timing,* New York City: Riverhead Books, 2019.

Printed in Great Britain
by Amazon